Britain and European Integration since 1945

B

Making Contemporary Britain

General Editor: Anthony Seldon
Consultant Editor: Peter Hennessy

Books in the series

Northern Ireland since 1968
Paul Arthur and Keith Jeffery

The Prime Minister since 1945
James Barber

British General Elections since 1945
David Butler

Britain and the Suez Crisis
David Carlton

The End of The British Empire
John Darwin

British Defence since 1945
Michael Dockrill

Britain and the Falklands War
Lawrence Freedman

Britain and European Integration since 1945
Stephen George

Consensus Politics from Attlee to Thatcher
Dennis Kavanagh and Peter Morris

Women in Britain since 1945
Jane Lewis

Britain and the Korean War
Callum MacDonald

Culture in Britain since 1945
Arthur Marwick

Crime and Criminal Justice since 1945
Terence Morris

The British Press and Broadcasting since 1945
Colin Seymour-Ure

British Science and Politics since 1945
Tom Wilkie

British Public Opinion
Robert M. Worcester

Institute of Contemporary British History
34 Tavistock Square, London WC1H 9EZ

Britain and European Integration since 1945

Stephen George

BLACKWELL
Oxford UK & Cambridge USA

Copyright © Stephen George 1991

First published 1991

Basil Blackwell Ltd
108 Cowley Road, Oxford, OX4 1JF, UK

Basil Blackwell, Inc.
3 Cambridge Center
Cambridge, Massachusetts 02142, USA

British Library Cataloguing in Publication Data

A CIP catalogue record for this book is available from the British Library.

Library of Congress Cataloging in Publication Data

George, Stephen.
   Britain and European Integration since 1945/Stephen George.
      p. cm. – (Making Contemporary Britain)
   ISBN 0-631-16894-X; 0-631-16895-8 (p/bk)
   1. European Economic Community – Great Britain. 2. Great Britain –
   Economic conditions – 1945–3. Europe – Economic integration.
   4. Europe 1992. 5. e-uk e.   I. Title. II. Series
HF1534.5.E9G46 1991
337.1'42 – dc20   90-23125
                                                                  CIP

Typeset in 11 on 13 pt Ehrhardt
by Setrite Typesetters Ltd
Printed in Great Britain by Billing & Sons Ltd., Worcester

Contents

General Editor's Preface

The Institute of Contemporary British History's series *Making Contemporary Britain* is aimed directly at students and at others interested in learning more about topics in post-war British history. In the series, authors are less attempting to break new ground than presenting clear and balanced overviews of the state of knowledge on each of the topics.

The ICBH was founded in October 1986 with the objective of promoting the study of British history since 1945 at every level. To that end, it publishes books and a quarterly journal, *Contemporary Record*; it organizes seminars and conferences for school students, undergraduates, researchers and teachers of post-war history; and it runs a number of research programmes and other activities.

A central theme of the ICBH's work is that post-war history is too often neglected in British schools, institutes of higher education and beyond. The ICBH acknowledges the validity of the arguments against the study of recent history, notably the problems of bias, overly subjective teaching and writing, and the difficulties of perspective. But it believes that the values of studying post-war history outweigh the drawbacks, and that the health and future of a liberal democracy require that its citizens know more about the most recent past of their country than the limited knowledge possessed by British citizens, young and old, today. Indeed, the ICBH believes that the dangers of political indoctrination are higher where the young are not informed of the recent past.

There could not be a more appropriate moment than the present for Stephen George's book to appear, with Britain becoming ever more associated with her European partners throughout the 1990s.

Many critical, historical and contemporary questions are tackled head on. Why did Britain stand aloof from Europe in the 1950s, and then make a volte face in the 1960s, only to have her application to join the EEC rejected twice? Did Britain lose out by not joining until 1973? What have been the gains and losses to Britain of entry since?

George's analysis is well-informed and succinct. By setting the debate over Europe in its historical context, he provides an important service to readers. This short book deserves to be widely read.

Anthony Seldon

Preface

Britain has been a member of the European Community (EC) since 1973, but it is only recently, with the publicity surrounding the '1992' campaign and the role of the EC in such areas as social and environmental policy, that many British people have fully realized what membership means and, more importantly perhaps, what it might mean in the not-too-distant future. Although successive British governments have attempted to block the evolution of the EC into a federal European structure, and have consistently played down that side of what the EC is about, the fact is that a process of European integration is in train, and Britain is being carried along inexorably with it. It is the view of the author that that process will prove most significant in the making of contemporary Britain before the turn of the century.

This book begins with a history of the process of European integration in chapter 1, before turning to look at the attitude of British governments in chapter 2, and the domestic political dimension of participation in the process in chapter 3. Chapter 4 offers a brief survey of some of the effects on Britain of its membership of the EC.

Writing contemporary history is notoriously fraught with problems, one of which is knowing where to stop; because, of course, history itself does not stop, and the temptation is always to try to take account of the most recent twists in the story. Even so, I have avoided entering into too much discussion of the momentous events that occurred in Eastern Europe in the later months of 1989, because they really were too recent to gain any sort of perspective on them at all. This explains why these undoubtedly significant events are mentioned only briefly.

I would like to record my thanks to Andrew Gamble and Ben Rosamond for their comments on the first draft of chapter 3: I did not incorporate all of their suggestions, so the weaknesses that remain are entirely my own. Anthony Seldon and an anonymous referee read the whole typescript, but they too are exonerated of any responsibility for my mistakes.

Stephen George
Department of Politics
University of Sheffield

Abbreviations

EC	European Communities/European Community
ECSC	European Coal and Steel Community
Ecu	European currency unit
EDC	European Defence Community
EEC	European Economic Community
EFTA	European Free Trade Association
EMS	European Monetary System
EPC	European Political Co-operation
Euratom	European Atomic Energy Community
GATT	General Agreement on Tariffs and Trade
IMF	International Monetary Fund
NATO	North Atlantic Treaty Organization
OEEC	Organization for European Economic Co-operation
SDP	Social Democratic Party
OPEC	Organization of Petroleum Exporting Countries
UEF	Union Européenne des Fédéralistes
WEU	Western European Union

1 European Integration

In Britain the term 'European integration' is usually taken to refer to the integration of national economies. It is true that it is in the realm of economics that integration has made the greatest advances in post-war Europe. But for many Europeans outside of Britain, economic integration is only one aspect of a wider process that will eventually involve the integration of national political systems. Economics may lead the way at present, but the process of European integration could well lead to a Europe united on federal principles, with a clear division of responsibilities between the states and the central federal authorities, and a distinct federal political system existing alongside, though separate from, national systems.

Immediately after the Second World War there was a strong movement for the creation of such a united Europe, to remove the risk of another war starting from national divisions in the Continent. Initially the demand was pressed by federalist groups which had grown up in the resistance movements of occupied Europe, and which looked for the immediate creation of a federal constitution for the Continent. The disappointment of these hopes left the field open to other initiatives, one of which, a process of integration by sectors, formed the basis for the setting up of the European Communities (EC) which gradually came to be the most important vehicle of European unity, although other organizations continued to play a role.

The federalist movement

During the Second World War the idea of European unity, which had been around for many years, gained considerable support in the resistance movements of continental western Europe. The resistance fighters believed that they were fighting an ideological war, not a national war. French resistance fighters fought not only German occupiers, but also Vichy French; Italian partisans fought Italian fascists; in many other countries the war was fought between people of the same nationality.

Nationalism itself was an ideology that had been expropriated by the fascists and Nazis, and had become discredited in the adoption. For the resistance fighters, whether communist, socialist, or Roman Catholic, the lesson of the war was the necessity to supersede the nation state in the post-war Europe that would emerge (Lipgens, 1982, pp. 44–58).

In December 1946 some of the most committed federalists, many of them resistance leaders, came together to form the European Union of Federalists (Union Européenne des Fédéralistes – UEF). Their aim was to establish a federal united states of Europe: their strategy was to move simply and dramatically to establish a constitution for a federal Europe (Harrison, 1974, p. 47). That did not seem absurdly naive in the immediate aftermath of a war which had displaced the old national political elites and turned the structure of Europe upside down.

Unfortunately for the UEF, the very disruption that had created the possibility of a new start hindered rapid convening of the necessary constitutional convention. By the time that a Congress was convened, in May 1948 in The Hague, the old political structures had already been re-erected. National government had been restored throughout the Continent.

There was some public sympathy for the federal cause, and at the Hague Congress important national political figures, including the British wartime leader Winston Churchill, spoke in favour of European unity. But words are cheap, and when the time came to turn them into action the commitment was less evident.

The Council of Europe

The Hague Congress led directly to the creation of the Council of Europe, which still exists today as a 23−nation body that performs valuable work in bringing together parliamentarians to exchange views and to pursue investigations into matters of common concern, such as environmental questions.

It was in the Council of Europe that agreement was reached on a European Convention on Human Rights; and both the European Commission of Human Rights, which monitors compliance with the terms of the Convention by signatory states, and the European Court of Human Rights, which adjudicates on charges of violation, are institutions of the Council of Europe.

At the end of the 1980s the Council seemed to be about to take on a new role as a forum in which the states of Eastern Europe would be able to start working alongside those of Western Europe on practical issues. But despite still having a role to play in the quest for European unity, the Council is not even an embryonic federal government for Europe. That aspiration was killed off early in its history, largely by Britain.

When the Labour Government of Clement Attlee declared that it was not about to assist in the creation of a federal Europe, the federalists consoled themselves with the argument that the Conservatives would soon return to office in Britain, and then Churchill would reverse the policy. In October 1951 the Conservatives did return to office. However in late November of that year Sir David Maxwell Fyfe, the Home Secretary and a renowned pro-European, was telling the Assembly of the Council that Britain could not go along with the schemes that were being hatched to develop the Council into a European government.

Paul-Henri Spaak, the Belgian Foreign Minister and a convinced advocate of European union, recorded in his memoirs the dismay that was caused by that statement (Spaak, 1971, pp. 219−22). It was clear that the constitutional strategy had failed. Where should the federalists turn next?

Functional integration

An alternative approach to integration, by functional economic steps rather than by a full frontal assault on political sovereignty, had already been suggested by the setting up in April 1948 of the Organization for European Economic Co-operation (OEEC). Originally OEEC was the co-ordinating agency for the distribution of money that the United States contributed to the economic reconstruction of Western Europe through its European Recovery Program ('Marshall Aid' as it was commonly known). The US Administration insisted that the use of the funds be organized by the Europeans themselves on an international basis. This stipulation was designed to encourage European unity, which the United States strongly advocated as the key to a prosperous and stable Western Europe. In the event, OEEC never achieved this objective; like the Council of Europe it was never to develop beyond inter-governmentalism. Once its task with respect to Marshall Aid was complete, it devoted itself to attempting to reduce restrictions on trade between member states, and monitoring the prospects for their economic growth. In 1961 it was replaced by the Organization for Economic Co-operation and Development (OECD), the membership of which went beyond Europe to include the United States and Canada. Today, OECD has over 20 member states and continues to perform a useful function as one of several institutions for the co-ordination of national economic policies.

Although OEEC did not prove to be a decisive step towards European unity, it did point the way to the functional route which was later to be adopted as the basis for the European Coal and Steel Community (ECSC), the precursor of the EC. As Urwin (1981, p. 143) says, 'The founders of the ECSC and the Common Market undoubtedly learnt some important lessons from the functioning of OEEC.'

One of the key founders of ECSC was Jean Monnet, a French civil servant who had been charged with the task of planning the reconstruction of French industry in the aftermath of the war. He was not exactly a federalist, but he did come to realize that French industry would not be able to operate at the most efficient level of production unless it had access to a market larger than that of France alone. What was needed was'a vast continental market on a European scale' (Monnet, 1963, p. 205). In this respect Monnet was an advocate of European unity, although his primary concern was not the creation of a European government but the creation of a European economy. Underlying this concern was something that was to figure prominently in French attitudes to European integration: an awareness of the need for European companies to have a domestic market larger than any single state, to allow them to expand production to the optimum scale and to compete with US companies, which already had a continental-scale domestic market. Rivalry with the Americans strongly influenced French thinking on this matter.

Monnet advocated integration by sectors. If governments could surrender their sovereign control over just one or two industrial sectors, they would soon come to appreciate the advantages of co-ordinated planning, and could be persuaded to surrender control over other sectors. Gradually, without ever making a decision to do so, they would create a European economy by piecemeal surrender of control, sector by sector.

The two sectors chosen to start the process were coal and steel. These were both industries with problems that could more readily be solved at a supranational than national level. Coal was in short supply in Europe in 1950, steel in excess. A European body would be able to ensure that the available supplies of coal were equitably distributed, and that overcapacity in the steel industry was neutralized by a fair system of general restraint on production (Diehold, 1959, pp. 16–20).

These general factors help to explain why the idea of a supranational coal and steel organization gained the acceptance of other governments. It was not so much a commitment to the ideal of supranational integration as a response to practical problems, that drove the process. In addition to the particular problems associated with the coal and steel industries, there were also important political reasons for West Germany and Italy to participate in the scheme. Germany in particular needed to live down its recent history and to re-establish itself as a member of the West European system of states. The same applied to Italy, if to a lesser extent; and the Italian Christian Democrat leaders had the added incentive of wanting to tie the country into the capitalist system as firmly as possible, in the context of a domestic political situation where the Communists formed the second largest party.

For France, too, practical considerations may have counted for more than federalist ideals, or even the sense of rivalry with the United States. Alan Milward has stressed the extent to which the success of Monnet's modernization plan for the French economy depended on France gaining access to German supplies of coal and coke from the Ruhr region, and also on French steel not being driven out of export markets by competition from reviving German industry. To Milward it is clear that 'The Schuman Plan was invented to safeguard the Monnet Plan' (Milward, 1984, p. 395).

Milward has also contested the generally accepted story of the genesis of the scheme, that it was hatched entirely within Monnet's *Commissariat du Plan*, and that Monnet then put his ideas to the French Foreign Minister, Robert Schuman, who adopted them enthusiastically. Milward (1984, pp. 395−6) argues that the French Ministry of Foreign Affairs also played an important role in the genesis and development of the idea. Certainly the scheme served an important objective of French foreign policy, tying the new German state into an arrangement that would make it difficult for it to threaten France militarily. The need to control the power of Germany, to prevent it dominating Europe either militarily or economically, was, and has remained, a constant theme of French policy.

Because the French Foreign Minister made public the plan for European states to pool their supplies of coal and steel under a common High Authority, the idea bears his name: the Schuman Plan. It was announced at a press conference on 9 May, 1950. Within a short space of time the governments of the Federal Republic of Germany, Belgium, The Netherlands, Luxembourg, and Italy had responded favourably. The British Government was invited to participate, but declined to do so.

At the negotiation stage the federalists pressed successfully for the setting up, alongside the High Authority, of a European Parliamentary Assembly, and the participating states insisted on a Council of Ministers representing their interests (Diebold, 1959, pp. 62–3). So the basic pattern of institutions that was to emerge in the European Community first appeared in the ECSC in 1952.

One step back: the European Defence Community

Looked at from the federalists' point of view, ECSC marked a big step forward towards a united Europe. Within a few years, though, the progress seemed to have been halted, and reversed, with the failure of the attempt to create a European Defence Community (EDC).

For those federalists who adopted the strategy of integration by functional sectors, the logic of the approach was that defence would be the last sector to be integrated. It was the sector where, more than any other sector, a movement away from national control would be seen as an attack on sovereignty. But world events put defence to the top of the agenda in 1950, when North Korean troops invaded South Korea.

Korea, like Germany, was divided at the end of the war into communist and capitalist states. The invasion of the capitalist Korea by the communist Korea was interpreted in the West as a sign that the communist world was intent on expansion, and this focused concern on Germany. The United States was prepared to commit a large contingent of troops to the defence of South Korea, under the banner of the United Nations; but it insisted that Western Europe provide more for its own defence, thus taking some of the burden off US shoulders. In particular, it began to demand that the Federal Republic of Germany should contribute to its own defence (Fursdon, 1980, pp. 67–80).

For France, this was an unacceptable demand. Three times in 70 years German troops had invaded French territory, and the demilitarization of Germany at the end of the war had been pressed vigorously by the French Government, which now resisted the emergence of a new German army. However, the French were not in a strong bargaining position, as their defence was also in question here, and they were clearly in no position to make up the extra European forces from their own reserves.

Under these circumstances, the French premier, René Pleven, proposed a scheme for the pooling of European military resources that copied the ECSC pooling of coal and steel resources. Monnet drew up the plan, despite his own reservations about its feasibility (Fursdon, 1980, pp. 86–90).

For the federalists the Pleven Plan for a European Defence Community (EDC) was an opportunity to revive their preferred strategy for a federal constitution. Through the forum of the Parliamentary Assembly of the ECSC, which was asked to look at the detail of the scheme, they argued that a European army was a highly political concept, and that the EDC should therefore be accompanied by a European Political Community. The argument was accepted, and the political community was incorporated in the treaty that was signed by the governments of the same six states that formed the ECSC (Urwin, 1981, pp. 175–6). But the treaty had a difficult passage when it was brought before national parliaments, an eventually, at the end of August 1954, it failed to gain ratification in France, where the scheme had been hatched, and so the EDC collapsed.

Western European Union

Britain, which had stood aloof from the EDC, now stepped in with an alternative suggestion for organizing European defence. The Prime Minister, Anthony Eden, proposed a Western European Union (WEU), which would group the six ECSC states with Britain in a system of mutual defence treaties. In this context a German army could be reconstituted, with France having the assurance that if it was ever turned against them, Britain would be treaty-bound to support the French.

WEU was an expansion of the Brussels Treaty of 1948. That treaty had been between Britain, France, and the Benelux states, and had been aimed primarily at giving a British military guarantee to the other states against renewed German aggression, thus paving the way for the eventual creation of the Federal Republic. But whereas the other signatories, and especially the French, were understandably concerned about Germany, the British Foreign Secretary Ernest Bevin was already of the view that the greater threat to peace in Europe came from the Soviet Union. For this reason his main objective was to tie the United States into a firm commitment to the defence of Western Europe, which was achieved by the signing of the North Atlantic Treaty on 4 April 1949, creating the North Atlantic Treaty Organization (NATO).

It seemed to some observers that the main significance of WEU was simply that it allowed Germany to join a traditional military alliance, and so paved the way for the entry of the Federal Republic into NATO. As Monnet put it, 'the rest was no more than a feeble co-ordinating structure doomed to a vegetative existence' (Monnet, 1978, p. 398).

But in 1966 President de Gaulle withdrew France from the integrated command structure of NATO, and after that WEU provided a forum in which the other European members of NATO were able to co-ordinate their NATO-determined strategy with France's independent strategy.

In the 1980s WEU came to take on another role. From the early 1980s there was consistent pressure for European defence co-operation to be intensified, in the face of US demands that the burden of defence be more equitably shared across the Atlantic, but also in the face of some rather alarming twists in US policy which left the European allies feeling that their interests were sometimes less influential in determining the direction of that policy than were domestic US political considerations. However, the reluctance of neutral Ireland to allow defence on to the EC agenda made WEU a useful alternative forum for co-ordinating the European response to shifts in US policy.

From ECSC to the Common Market

So far as the aspirations of the federalists for a united Europe were concerned, the collapse of EDC marked the second and final collapse of the constitutional strategy. From this point on, the strategy of integration by sectors was left with the field to itself.

Pursuing his original line of thought, Monnet in the mid-1950s suggested that atomic energy be made the next sector for integration. His idea was taken up by the French government, but at the same time an alternative idea was brought forward by the Benelux states. These countries — Belgium, The Netherlands, and Luxembourg — had formed an economic union at the end of the war. They had abolished tariff barriers in trade between themselves, and now proposed that this idea be applied to the whole of Western Europe, forming a general common market.

Monnet's scheme and the Benelux scheme went forward in tandem. As with the Schuman Plan, Britain was invited to participate. The British had long made it clear that they preferred economic co-operation to be handled through the inter-governmental OEEC. Nevertheless, the British Conservative Government did send an official to the early sessions of the Messina negotiations, at which the details of the two schemes were worked out; but the official was withdrawn at an early stage in the process — 'One day he disappeared and never came again' a Belgian official later recalled (Charlton, 1983, p. 191) — and the same six states were left to proceed together again.

Political events contributed to the rapid negotiation of treaties to form the two new Communities. The French war in Algeria was perhaps the most significant. It rapidly began to threaten the continued existence not just of particular French governments, but the whole Fourth Republic; the only person who seemed able to avert civil war in France looked increasingly to be General de Gaulle. But de Gaulle had spoken strongly against the ideal of European unity, and it was widely believed that he would put an end to France's participation in the Messina negotiations if and when he came to office. There thus developed what was afterwards described as 'the rush to Rome' (Laurent, 1972, p. 209); that is, the negotiating states speeded up their progress so as to get the treaties signed and ratified before the impending collapse of the existing pro-integration regime in France.

The Rome Treaties set up two new Communities: the European Atomic Energy Community (Euratom), and the European Economic Community (EEC). While ostensibly about economics, the preamble of the EEC Treaty made it clear that the objective was 'to lay the foundation of an ever closer union amongst the peoples of Europe'. What had been embarked upon was both an economic and a political exercise.

Although we now know that the EEC was to prove the major vehicle for European integration, it was not clear at the time that it would emerge as a more successful venture than Euratom, or indeed whether either would prove successful. It was not even clear that the future of European integration lay with the Communities at all. As Harold Macmillan recalled in his memoirs:

> when I was appointed Foreign Secretary in the spring of 1955, there seemed not one straight and simple road towards the objective of unity in Europe but several paths, sometimes parallel, sometimes crossing each other. Was the unit of co-operation to be extended into the concept of a North Atlantic Alliance? Was this to replace the European ideal? At the other extreme, was Europe, already partitioned between East and West, Communist and Free, to be again divided between the three great countries of the Western continent − France, Germany and Italy − with Holland, Belgium and Luxembourg at their side, and the rest, led by Britain? Was the economic future of Europe to lie in the OEEC, more comprehensive in its membership than even the Council of Europe, or was it to be based upon the Schuman concept ... ? (Macmillan, 1971, pp. 64−5)

It was the spectacular success of the EEC that was to resolve this issue, and make it into the main vehicle of European integration. That success overcame the division between the six and 'the rest, led by Britain' because it pushed Britain, and some of the rest, into joining the EEC. The other organizations mentioned by Macmillan, the Council of Europe and OEEC (now transformed into OECD), also continued to exist; and in the context of the 1990s, when the other division of Europe 'between East and West, Communist and Free' has also been overcome, they may have a new role to play. It seems unlikely, though, that they will displace the EC as the centrepiece of the new Europe.

The EC: institutional structure

Since the EC did eventually emerge as the main vehicle of European integration, it will be useful to outline very briefly its institutional structure. (For further detail see Nugent, 1989.)

The four main institutions are the Commission, the Council of Ministers, the European Parliament, and the European Court of Justice. Until 1967 the ECSC, Euratom, and the EEC, had separate Commissions (in the case of ECSC it was called the High Authority); but since 1967 there has been a single set of institutions for all three Communities.

The Commission consists of one nominee from each member state, plus a second nominee from the larger member states. In the original EC the larger member states were France, Germany, and Italy; so there were originally nine Commissioners. In 1973 Britain, Ireland, and Denmark joined the EC; in 1981 Greece became the tenth member state; and in 1986 Spain and Portugal brought the total membership to twelve. Of these later entrants, Britain and Spain counted as larger member states, having two Commissioners each; so by the end of the 1980s there were seventeen Commissioners.

These Commissioners are not national representatives. On taking office they swear not to press the national interest of their own or any other member state, but to act always in the interest of the EC as a whole. They are assisted by a small bureaucracy based in the famous Berlaymont building in Brussels.

The Commission is the only institution in the EC which can

make proposals for Community legislation. It has therefore been seen as the 'motor of integration'. It is also charged with the task of monitoring the compliance of member states with EC legislation, and reporting to the European Court of Justice any that do not fulfil their obligations.

Proposals for EC legislation go from the Commission to the Council of Ministers, which consists of national Government Ministers from all the member states. Which Ministers are involved depends on the subject under discussion: Agriculture Ministers when it is agricultural policy, Environment Ministers when it is environmental policy, and so on. At the summit of this system is the European Council, which consists of the Heads of Government (for France the Head of State), meeting at least twice a year.

Since its creation in 1974 the European Council has tended to set the agenda for future developments in the EC, thereby appearing to take over some of the Commission's function as initiator. This has the advantage that once the Heads of State and Government have agreed that progress ought to be made on a particular issue, there is more chance of getting proposals through the Council of Ministers than if the principles as well as the details had to be settled there. However, it remains the case that only the Commission can make specific proposals for EC legislation. The role of the European Council has been compared to that of a Borad of Directors of a company, setting the broad corporate objectives but leaving it to the management (in this case the Commission working with the Council of Ministers) to implement policy (Morgan, 1976).

Proposals from the Commission can only become EC law if accepted by the Council of Ministers, which makes it the effective legislature of the EC. For many years the Council of Ministers operated on a veto system, but in 1987 the Single European Act introduced a system of weighted majority voting for a limited range of legislation concerned specifically with removing non-tariff barriers to trade between the member states, in pursuit of the creation of a single EC market by the end of 1992.

The European Parliament, which has been directly elected

only since 1979, has a right to give its opinion on any proposal from the Commission; but the Council of Ministers was until 1987 able to ignore that opinion of it so wished. In 1987 the adoption of the Single European Act increased the powers of amendment of the European Parliament with respect to those items of legislation covered by the new rules on majority voting (Lodge, 1989). It also has some power over the process of setting the budget of the EC, and it can dismiss the Commission from office. It remains, however, a far less powerful institution than are national parliaments.

The European Court of Justice, which is looked at in chapter 4 below, adjudicates on charges that EC law has not been observed, and issues definitive rulings on the correct inter-pretation of EC law in national Courts.

The EEC: early success

To the surprise of many people, including most of the British establishment, the EEC proved to be remarkably successful. Within a few years of its foundation the member states had agreed on the level of their common external tariff for industrial imports, and had put in place the elements of a common agricultural policy.

These achievements were partly due to the adaptation of industry to the reality of the existence of the common market, partly to the skill of the Commission in manipulating the situation, and partly to the determination of the governments of the member states to make a success of the venture.

Adaptation by industrialists is most apparent in the attitude of French industry, which generally had opposed the setting up of the common market, fearing that it would lead to their home market being swamped by German industrial products. Once it became apparent that the market was going to come into existence, those same French industrialists responded to the challenge that they could no longer avoid by concluding joint production and marketing agreements with companies in other member states. Having geared themselves to the new situation, they then became impatient at the slow progress that was being made in actually bringing it about, and became one of the main pressure groups pressing for an acceleration of the originally agreed schedule for completing the common market. In May 1960 the member states reached agreement on an acceleration of this timetable in line with these demands (Lindberg, 1963, p. 171).

The role of the European Commission in the process was crucial. It acted as a broker between the conflicting interests of the member states, and also took full advantage of an implicit deal between Germany and France which linked the industrial common market, from which German industry would clearly benefit, with a common agricultural policy, from which French farmers would benefit. The Commission ensured that the pressure for progress on one front led always to progress on both fronts. In this process the diplomatic skills and leadership qualities of Walter Hallstein, the first President of the Commission, and of Sicco Mansholt, his senior Vice-President and the holder of the agricultural portfolio, were crucial (Coombes, 1970, p. 259).

Yet all the pressure from industrial and agricultural interests, and all of Hallstein's and Mansholt's skills, would have been in vain had it not been for the willingness of the member states to make a success of the EEC. Here the positions of two states were of key importance. One was France, which in 1958 came under the leadership of de Gaulle, as anticipated. It soon became apparent that de Gaulle had no intention of removing France from the new Communities, and that on the contrary he was favourably disposed to the argument that the EEC would make French industry more efficient, and therefore France richer, which in turn would enhance France's international prestige. The other state whose position was important was Britain. The open scepticism of the British political leadership about the prospects for success of the EEC made their counterparts in the six member states determined to prove them wrong.

De Gaulle's leadership bid

Not only did de Gaulle see the European Communities as means of ensuring the economic prosperity of France: he also saw the grouping of six states as a potential bloc in support of French foreign policy. For that reason he proposed, in July 1960, that the six member states institute amongst themselves a procedure for political co-operation. In line with de Gaulle's suspicions of supranationalism, and of what he saw as the ambition of the Commission of the EEC to become a European Government, this procedure was to operate alongside the institutional machinery of the Communities, but separate from it. The proposals were first formally tabled in November 1961 by de Gaulle's foreign minister, Christian Fouchet, and became known as the Fouchet Plan.

Co-operation on foreign policy was accompanied in this plan by proposals for co-operation in the scientific and cultural fields, the protection of human rights and democracy, and a common defence policy (Silj, 1967, p. 142). But it was on the issue of foreign policy co-operation that negotiations focused. The smaller member states, in particular, were suspicious of de Gaulle's motives, particularly when he began to develop close relations with the German Chancellor, Konrad Adenauer. It seemed to the Benelux states that France was intent on dominating foreign policy, and their response was to link progress on political co-operation with agreement on the admission to membership of Britain, which made an application in 1961. Negotiations on the Fouchet Plan broke down on 17 April 1962 because of the refusal of the Belgians and the Dutch to sign any treaty on political co-operation until Britain was a member of the EC (Bodenheimer, 1967, p. 64).

British membership was the last thing that de Gaulle wanted. With Britain in the EC there would be a rival leader, to which other states could rally in opposing French plans. At first he seems to have hoped that the British were not sufficiently serious about entry to accept the tough terms that the French insisted upon in the negotiations; then, when it became apparent that the British were determined, de Gaulle tried to separate membership of the EC from participation in the political co-operation plan, but the Benelux states were not prepared to accept that. Finally, in 1963, he simply vetoed British member-ship, arguing that Britain was not yet ready to accept a 'European vocation', and would act as a US Trojan horse inside the Communities.

This episode illustrated clearly the continuing Anglo-French dispute over the future of Europe. At its core was a difference over the relationship between the EC and the outside world, especially the United States. Since the late 1940s, France had pursued a policy of building up a West European grouping of states that would be independent of the United States, both economically and politically. In this respect de Gaulle's policy was in line with that of his predecessors, and it was acceptance of this view of the EC which de Gaulle made his test of Britain's 'European' credentials.

Shortly after the veto, de Gaulle and Adenauer signed a treaty of friendship between their two countries, which signified France's determination to enlist Germany as an ally in building the Europe that France wanted. Although the relationship has suffered considerable strain at times, not least over the issue of the Atlantic relationship itself, the Franco-German axis has remained a cornerstone of the EC ever since.

The crisis of 1965

France's unilateral veto of British membership was the most serious crisis that the EC had had to face up to that date. But within two years there developed a second and even more serious crisis, with significant implications for the future of European integration.

De Gaulle's idea of European unity was of a Europe of co-operating nation-states. He wanted economic integration, so that the French economy could partake of the benefits of a large market, but he always rejected the notion of political integration, which would erode the sovereignty of the separate states. It was this issue that was at the heart of the 1965 crisis.

By 1965 the first stage of economic integration was almost complete. The common external tariff was in place, and the detail of the common agricultural policy had been agreed. All that remained to be sorted out was the financing of the budget. Up to that point the budget of the EEC had been financed by contributions from the member states. The Commission, on 1 April 1965, proposed that there should be a shift to an automatic funding mechanism which would involve the revenue from the common external tariff and the levy on imported agricultural products becoming the EEC's 'own' resources. Member states would keep a percentage of tariffs to cover collection costs, but the rest would be remitted directly to Brussels.

In the course of the discussion in national parliaments of these proposals, the question was raised of democratic control over these funds which were to be transferred automatically to the EEC. The Dutch parliament in particular insisted that since national parliaments would no longer have budgetary control, the European Parliament ought to be given budgetary powers to ensure that there was a democratic review of executive decisions. This idea was taken up by the Commission and incorporated into the proposals for definitive financing of the budget that went to the Council of Ministers (Holt, 1973, p. 68).

Giving budgetary powers to the European Parliament was a step towards supranationalism, and was unacceptable to de Gaulle. The French response startled the Commission and the other member states. Before all the negotiating process was completed, de Gaulle withdrew the French representative, and from 6 July 1965 France boycotted all meetings of the Council of Ministers, thereby effectively blocking any progress.

A settlement of this crisis was eventually reached in the early part of 1966, in negotiations that took place in Luxembourg. At this point it became clearer why de Gaulle had acted so precipitately, provoking the crisis, because the major issue on which France demanded concessions was not the powers of the European Parliament at all, but the transition to majority voting that would, according to the Treaty of Rome, take place once the first stage of integration was completed. This formed a more serious and fundamental challenge to national sovereignty, because up to that point every state had the right to veto proposals which it did not like, whereas under the majority-voting system an individual state could be outvoted, and have forced upon it proposals which it found unacceptable.

In the so-called 'Luxembourg compromise' it was agreed by all the member states that if any state considered a proposal posed a threat to its vital national interests, it could exercise a veto, even after the notional transition to majority voting had taken place. This agreement had no status in Community law, but was more in the way of a 'gentlemen's agreement' not to force any member of the club into a position which it found impossible to live with. Despite its informal nature, it rapidly became established as a mechanism for vetoing majority voting on a whole range of issues, many of which could only very loosely be described as vital national interests.

There were other concessions that de Gaulle demanded as his price for re-entering the Council. For example, he insisted that control of EEC publicity be taken out of the hands of the Commission, a response to anti-Gaullist comment in official publications; and that ambassadors to the Communities from non-member states should present their credentials to the President of the Commission and to the President of the Council at the same time, rather than just to the President of the Commission (Holt, 1973, pp. 71–2). These were symbolic moves, but they contributed to a sense of humiliation that spread rapidly within the Commission in the aftermath of the crisis, and which led to a collapse of morale that weakened the campaigning role of the Commission as a promoter of integration for some years to come.

On the issue that was ostensibly the cause of the crisis, the financing of the budget, no agreement was reached in 1966. The common agricultural policy came into operation, but the budget was still funded from annually negotiated national contributions. No change was made in this until after de Gaulle's retirement in 1969; and British entry, for which a renewed application was made by Harold Wilson's Labour Government in 1967, also had to wait, as de Gaulle immediately exercised his veto in reply to the renewed application.

After de Gaulle: the relaunching of European integration

Georges Pompidou, who had been the French Prime Minister during much of de Gaulle's presidency, won the presidential election in France in June 1969, and soon afterwards called for the convening of a summit conference of the leaders of the EC member states to discuss the relaunching of European integration. The summit was held in The Hague.

Pompidou's motive for taking this step is not entirely clear, although such a conference had already been publicly suggested by the German Chancellor, Willy Brandt, while the French election was still in progress, and the need for the issue of enlargement to be reconsidered was pressed on the new President by his partners in the first weeks after his election (Kitzinger, 1973, p. 69). It has also been suggested that the summit was imposed on him by the small parties in the centre of the French political spectrum as the price for supporting him in the presidential election, or for supporting him in the French parliament (Kitzinger, 1973, p. 62).

Possibly there were economic reasons for the decision, too. After a period of rapid expansion in the early 1960s, the French economy had run into difficulties in the late sixties, which had contributed to de Gaulle's departure. In order to get the engine of growth going again, Pompidou devalued the franc, something that de Gaulle had refused to do because he saw it as a sign of national weakness. The objective of the devaluation was to make French exports more competitive. To widen the market for those exports, Pompidou was prepared to take another step that de Gaulle had refused to take, and agree to open negotiations for British entry to the EC.

However, Pompidou was keen that before Britain became a member, the issue of the financing of the EC budget should be settled. Although de Gaulle had rejected the Commission's 1965 proposals because of the element of supranationalism involved in increasing the budgetary powers of the EP, the terms were quite favourable to France, making it likely that she would be a net beneficiary from the system (Kitzinger, 1973, p. 74). On the other hand, it was clear that the same terms would be less beneficial in their effect on Britain, so unless the issue were settled before British entry the whole negotiation would be reopened, and the outcome would quite possibly be less favourable to France.

This, then, was the first agreement reached at The Hague: the completion of the first stage of integration. Linked to it in a scarcely concealed trade-off was the second agreement: to reopen negotiations with Britain and the other applicants for membership (Denmark, Ireland, and Norway) with a view to achieving enlargement of the Communities.

A third line of progress was agreed at The Hague, to add to these two items of left-over business from the past, and that was a major step forward into the future. All the leaders of the member states agreed to the objective of economic and monetary union by 1980. Economic union meant the establishment of common policies on economic management for all the EC; monetary union meant a single European currency, or at least a system that irrevocably tied together the rates of exchange of existing national currencies.

For France the more appealing part of this package was monetary union. If the German central bank, the Bundesbank, which had considerable foreign currency reserves as a consequence of the Federal Republic's large trade surpluses, could be persuaded to guarantee the value of the franc, the French currency would not come under the type of downward pressure from speculators that had made management of the exchange rate so difficult during the latter years of de Gaulle's presidency. The Germans, however, were not prepared to underwrite the French currency, or that of any other state, unless they had some voice in the economic policies that the other state would follow. Otherwise, they feared that they would be picking up the bill for policies that would allow rapid increases in the standard of living of the other state, unsustained by soundly-based economic growth. The compromise arrived at between these two positions was to progress on both fronts simultaneously, strengthening the economic co-ordination activities of the EC's existing Economic Policy Committees, and introducing a system that would tie the exchange rates of the currencies of the member states within narrow bands of fluctuation (Tsoukalis, 1977, pp. 90–8).

The Hague summit, then, agreed on a three-stage package of measures designed to move European integration forward: completion of the first stage of integration with agreement on financing the budget; widening the geographical coverage of the EC by opening negotiations for the entry of Britain, Ireland, Denmark and Norway; and deepening the level of integration through progress on economic and monetary union.

It did not take long to settle the question of financing the budget, thus clearing the way for enlargement. At the opening of the talks on British entry, Anthony Barber, at that time Britain's chief negotiator, made clear his unhappiness that this budgetary agreement had been reached without British participation, and his awareness that the agreed system would cause difficulties for Britain after entry (Barker, 1971, p. 247). But the British Government was not prepared to let this problem stand in the way of reaching agreement on the terms of entry.

Success in the negotiations on British entry was helped by the strong commitment shown by the British Prime Minister, Edward Heath. His attitude was that entry had been too long delayed, that the most important objective was to gain entry, and that other problems could then be sorted out from the inside. Even so, it took eighteen months of negotiation before terms could be agreed. Britain finally became a member of the EC on 1 January 1973, along with Ireland and Denmark; Norway agreed terms of entry, but membership was rejected by the Norwegian people in a referendum.

On two of the three objectives agreed at The Hague, then, the EC was successful. The third, economic and monetary union, was more ambitious, and in it the EC was less successful. As a result of the 'Barre Report', produced by Raymond Barre, the Commissioner responsible for monetary affairs, a system was set up known as 'the snake in the tunnel'. This was an arrangement whereby the exchange rates of the currencies of the member states were tied together within narrow bands of fluctuation (the top and bottom bands forming the 'tunnel', the fluctuation in the value of a currency between the top and bottom of the tunnel producing the 'snake'), and they jointly varied against the value of the dollar (Tsoukalis, 1977, p. 94).

The snake had a short life. It was torn apart by growing turbulence in the international monetary system, which led to rapid movements of speculative funds across exchanges, bringing one currency after another under downward or upward pressure. By the time that Britain entered the EC at the start of 1973 the French franc and Italian lira had already been forced out of the system. Sterling had also been a member of the snake, briefly, in 1972, but the Bank of England could not hold its parity and had had to withdraw.

By 1974 the turbulence in financial markets had been replaced as the main barrier to a successful joint float by the effects of the rise in the price of oil that took place in December 1973. The quadrupling of oil prices by the Organization of Petroleum Exporting Countries (OPEC) plunged the capitalist world into deep recession, but the effect on different national economies varied according to their underlying strength before the crisis. Few of the EC member states were able to match the level of performance of the West German economy, and consequently the snake lost one participant after another, until by 1977 it consisted of only five EC states plus two non-EC 'guest' participants (Sweden and Norway). It had become in effect a Deutschemark zone, providing stability to trade between the participants, but was no longer a vehicle to economic and monetary union for the EC.

The barren decade: 1974 to 1984

It took the EC a long time to settle all the outstanding issues left over from the enlargement negotiations. The main problems concerned Britain. First, because entry had become an issue in domestic British politics (see chapter 3 below), when there was a change of government in Britain the terms of entry had to be renegotiated. Scarcely was this episode finished than the effects on Britain of the budgetary arrangements came to dominate the agenda, as the transitional period of British membership came to an end and the full cost became apparent. So for most of the ten years from 1974 to 1984 the adaptation of Britain to the EC, and of the EC to British membership, dominated Community affairs, at the expense of further integration.

Perhaps, though, it is a little unfair to place the blame entirely on Britain, as some European observers were tempted to do. The decade was also one of economic recession, marked by a dramatic divergence in the performance of different national economies, which would have made any successful steps towards closer integration problematical even had Britain not had grievances to press (Hodges & Wallace, 1981; Hu, 1981). The suggestion that the domination of the EC's agenda by the various manifestations of the British problem crowded out other initiatives, which would have led to closer integration, presumes rather too easily that other issues were bidding to get on to the agenda. In fact, there is little to suggest that they were. With two marked exceptions this was a period when European integration stagnated because the conditions for furthering it were unfavourable. Even had Britain never joined the EC, it is difficult to see that there would have been much progress in the face of economic divergence.

The two exceptions to the general record of stagnation were European Political Co-operation (EPC) and the launching of the European Monetary System (EMS).

EPC was essentially a revival of de Gaulle's proposals for co-operation on foreign policy. These were more acceptable to the Benelux states once Britain was a member of the EC, thereby reducing the possibility of French domination of the process. Britain had always been positive about the idea, provided Britain were involved, and went along with the French view that the process should be parallel to the economic processes of the

EC, but should lie outside of the formal decision-making procedures of the Community.

This distinction was maintained in the early years of EPC's operation, but began to be increasingly difficult to sustain. The height of absurdity was reached when in November 1973 the Foreign Ministers of the nine member states met in Copenhagen one morning under the EPC heading, and then flew to Brussels to meet in the afternoon of the same day as the EC Council of Ministers. It was necessity, though, rather than ridicule, which eroded the distinction. In 1974, following the OPEC increase in the price of oil, the EC set up what became known as the 'Euro-Arab' dialogue with the Arab states. The Arab participants insisted on maintaining a clear linkage between trade and political questions, which forced the EC to respond by fudging the lines of demarcation between these areas on its side. Once the artificial distinction had broken down in this forum it was soon abandoned in practice in the Community's foreign policy dealings more generally. The Commission, originally excluded from meetings under EPC, is now involved in them at all levels, and has a vital co-ordinating role between EPC and economic external relations.

EPC had successes to show in a number of fields throughout the 1970s and into the 1980s. The Euro-Arab dialogue, despite some problems, set relations between these two highly interdependent parts of the world on a sounder footing than previously. In the Conference on Security and Co-operation in Europe in Helsinki in 1975, and in the various follow-up conferences, the EC states played a leading role in setting the agenda and influencing the outcomes through speaking with one voice. A growing proportion of decisions in the United Nations General Assembly were taken jointly by the member states, and other groups of states clearly adjusted their voting intentions in the light of the unified European line. In Latin America too, the EC states took an approach that was independent of and different from that of the United States, something that it would be difficult to believe any single state could have sustained alone against US pressure.

The EMS must also be judged a success. It resulted from a surprising initiative in 1978 by the German Chancellor, Helmut Schmidt, backed by the French President Valéry Giscard d'Estaing, to relaunch the idea of tying together the exchange rates of the currencies of the member states. That the system was able to work this time owed a great deal to the surprising weakness of the Deutschemark in the early years of its operation. Partly this weakness was a reflection of the strength of the dollar, buoyed up by high US interest rates; partly it was a reflection of the damage to the West German balance of payments caused by the second big rise in the price of oil, which took place in 1979. Both factors made it easier for the other members to maintain their parities with the Deutschemark whilst they worked at bringing down their rates of inflation to the German level. This step was essential to the long-term prospects for keeping the values of the currencies stable, and it was no longer the controversial issue it had been in 1969—72, because the inflationary effects of the increased oil prices had convinced all governments that lowering inflation had to be the main objective of economic policy. Although there was a spate of revaluations of currencies within the system in the early 1980s, the structure as a whole remained intact, and ensured the existence of a zone of monetary stability within the EC (Ludlow, 1982; Statler, 1979; Story, 1988).

There was only one exception to this record of success for the EMS. Britain chose not to become a full member of the system. The pound sterling was included in the basket of currencies that determined the value of the European currency unit (Ecu), the notional central currency to the value of which all the others were related; but Britain would not agree to set the value of the pound against the Ecu and maintain it through the exchange rate mechanism.

The 1980s: enlargement and relaunch

The EC started the 1980s still in rather poor condition. The agenda was dominated by an internal dispute, and by the issue of further enlargement. Ironically, the internal dispute was a still unresolved legacy of the first enlargement: it concerned the size of British net contributions to the common budget. Yet despite the difficulties that had resulted from admitting new members, in 1979 agreement was reached on Greece becoming the tenth member in 1981, and the applications of Spain and Portugal were being seriously entertained.

Political and strategic considerations, more than economics, lay behind the second enlargement. All three of the new applicants had recently been dictatorships, but had returned to democracy. The democratic political leaders in all three states saw EC membership as a means of guaranteeing the continuation of democracy. Only democracies could be members of the EC, and any member state which ceased to be democratic would cease to be a member. Given that membership would lead to a rapid growth of the interdependence of the national economy with the EC, it was believed that expulsion would soon become economically disastrous, making it practically impossible for any future dictatorship to survive. In addition, in both Greece and Spain there was a degree of hostility towards the United States because of the links it had had with the previous dictatorships; while in the case of Portugal, the role of left-wing army officers in the overthrow of the Caetano regime had meant that ideas for a neutral position in the capitalist-communist conflict in Europe were being taken seriously. By accepting the three states into membership, the EC was therefore taking an important step in ensuring that their loyalties remained with the West, and especially in the case of Greece in ensuring that influence could be brought to bear for that state to remain within NATO (George, 1985, pp. 154–66).

Greece became a member of the EC in 1981, and by 1984 negotiations on the entry of Spain and Portugal were complete. Also in 1984 the dispute over the size of British contributions to the EC budget was settled at the Fontainebleau European Council. Thus by the mid-1980s the agenda was clear for new initiatives. This was probably no coincidence, because concern had been growing since the start of the 1980s about the slow pace of Western Europe's recovery from recession.

The economic downturn provoked by the second oil crisis of 1979 hit the whole of the capitalist world, but within two years the Japanese and US economies had begun to grow rapidly again, whereas the EC remained in recession, with high unemployment and low growth (Pelkmans and Winters, 1988, p. 6). In West Germany there was growing disillusionment with the poor performance of the EC, and public opinion began to turn strongly in favour of developing closer relations with Eastern Europe, and particularly with the German Democratic Republic (East Germany).

It was this concern that primarily lay behind the 1981 initiative by the West German Foreign Minister, Hans Dietrich Genscher, for the negotiation of a new EC treaty that would strengthen the powers of the central institutions at the expense of those of the member states. It was pointed out by Genscher that the inability of the EC to move forward successfully owed much to the retention by national governments of a right of veto over all proposals for common action. With the enlargement of the EC to twelve members, that problem would be exacerbated at a time when it was vitally important for the future economic well-being of the member states that common decisions should be made to relaunch the experiment in integration.

Italy quickly rallied to this plan, and the Italian Foreign Minister, Emilio Colombo, put his name to what then became the Genscher-Colombo plan, prior to its being considered at a European Council meeting of the Heads of Government in London in November 1981. That European Council asked the Council of Foreign Ministers to consider the proposals, a process that eventually resulted in a Solemn Declaration on European Union at the Stuttgart European Council in June 1983. Although the Declaration fell short of being a new European Act, which was what had been proposed by Genscher and Colombo, it was accompanied by a plan of action to relaunch the process of European integration by tackling the immediate problems facing the EC and laying the basis for its further development. Momentum was given to the movement for reform of the EC system of making decisions by another Italian, Altiero Spinelli, a member of the European Parliament, on whose initiative the Parliament adopted a Draft Treaty on European Union in February 1984 (Lodge, 1986).

What eventually came out of this movement was the Single European Act of 1986. This Act guaranteed majority voting in the Council of Ministers of the EC for a range of specified measures, and increased the powers of amendment of the European Parliament for legislation under these headings. The measures covered by the new procedures were all concerned with the freeing of the internal market of the Community. This involved a range of reforms concerned with removing non-tariff barriers to trade, which had proliferated during the years of recession, and with extending the principle of free trade to service industries, particularly financial services.

For the most committed supporters of integration, the changes made in the Single European Act did not go nearly far enough. They certainly fell far short of the European Parliament's Draft Treaty. It seemed that what had been accepted was only the degree of reform necessary to allow the freeing of the market to proceed rapidly. This was a commonly accepted objective of the member states, all of whom were keenly aware both of the degree to which the EC was losing its competitive edge relative to Japan and the United States, and of the clearly expressed view of the European Round Table of Industrialists that the freeing of the internal market was the essential prerequisite for a renewal of investment (Pelkmans and Winters, 1988, p. 6).

Even within the programme for freeing the internal market there were areas of less than total agreement. France in particular was keen that the freeing of the market should be accompanied by rapid progress towards economic and monetary union, a prospect that was greeted less enthusiastically by Britain. And there was disagreement between Britain and most of the other member states on whether the economic measures should be accompanied by a 'social dimension' that would guarantee certain rights to workers in respect to wages, social security benefits, health and safety at work, and consultation on management decisions.

There was also a continuing tension amongst the member states between those like Italy and (according to public statements by President Mitterrand) France, which supported even more far-reaching institutional changes than those already introduced in the Single European Act, and those led by Britain, but including also Denmark and Greece, which were suspicious of European federalism and were anxious to make the minimum surrender of sovereignty compatible with achieving the free internal market.

A new dimension was given to this debate following the accession to office in the Soviet Union of the reformist Mikhail Gorbachev. His programme for restructuring the Soviet economy and developing better relations with the West led to a relaxation of Moscow's grip on the states of Eastern Europe, opening up new economic opportunities for the EC, but also raising difficult issues about the relationship of these states to the EC; and most worrying of all, German reunification became, first, a real possibility, and then increasingly a certainty.

This was how the situation stood at the end of the 1980s, with the rapid pace of change in Eastern Europe feeding ever more insistently into the discussion. Mitterrand and Delors treated the developments as evidence that the process of internal EC integration needed to be accelerated, otherwise the Community would be fragmented and possibly torn apart by the effort of responding. The British Government, however, read the opposite lesson into the freeing of Eastern Europe, arguing that too close unity within the EC would leave the East Europeans out in the cold and risk impeding their progress to democratic rule.

This was not the first time that British policy on Europe had failed to coincide with that of its EC partners. The history of the policy of successive British governments to the EC is the subject of the next chapter.

Conclusion

Initially the push for integration in post-war Europe came from the federalists, whose ideas had flourished in the resistance movements; but their attempt to achieve a new constitutional order was foiled by the reluctance of national political elites to give up sovereign powers once these were restored. It was Britain that finally delivered the death-blow to any hope that the Council of Europe might develop into a federal European government.

The constitutional strategy took on a new lease of life briefly when the plan for the EDC surfaced in the wake of the Korean war, but collapsed again when the necessary treaty failed to receive ratification from the French parliament. From that point on, the dominant strategy for European integration was the gradualist approach which Jean Monnet had already incorporated into the ECSC, and which subsequently produced Euratom and the EEC.

While these functional steps were supported by those who wanted to see a united Europe, they were taken by the national governments as responses to practical problems. But there was a consistency in the approach of successive French governments: they aimed to tie Germany into an inextricable web of functional agreements, and to create a European market that would both facilitate the recovery of the French economy, and allow Europe to emerge from its economic domination by the United States.

The EEC proved to be a successful experiment, and within a few years of its starting, other states were applying to join, most prominently Britain. This caused some dissension amongst the original six because of the opposition of President de Gaulle to admitting Britain, and enlargement was not finally achieved until 1973, by which time the favourable economic circumstances that had prevailed during the early years of the existence of the EEC began to change rapidly. From the mid-1970s to the mid-1980s the EC struggled to make progress, becoming bogged down in internal wrangles, although there were some advances in integration, notably the setting up of the EMS.

By the mid-1980s, with one further enlargement having taken membership to ten states and another imminent which would bring the total to twelve, there was a growing feeling that changes in the decision-making process would have to take place if the EC were not to become too unwieldy to make any progress at all. Added to this was serious concern about the sluggish performance of the European economy in comparison with Japan and the United States, which led directly to the launching of the programme to create a single internal market within the EC by the end of 1992.

By the end of the 1980s the single-market project had gathered considerable momentum, and was looking irreversible. But there were serious disagreements about how far the process needed to be taken, and the British Government, not for the first time since membership, appeared to be in direct conflict with most of the rest of the membership. This apparent awkwardness of the British has been seen as a contributory factor in explaining the poor record on integration in the 1970s, and has also been seen as a possible check on integration in the 1990s. The next two chapters look at the explanation for this record of British governments, first in terms of the overall foreign policy of the British State, and then in terms of the influence of domestic party-political considerations on policy towards the EC.

To help the reader keep the history detailed in this chapter in mind while reading the following chapter, the chronology of events on pp. 107–108 summarizes the major events.

2 The Policy of the British State

The previous chapter outlined the history of post-war attempts to integrate Western Europe. In this chapter the attitude of the British State to those developments will be examined. The underlying argument of the chapter is that there is a consistency in policy that is detectable across changes of government, and that the predominant factor influencing the policy of all British governments has been to ensure that the process of European integration did not result in a European regionalism that would disrupt the wider international world order. This commitment to a wider world order is here referred to as 'globalism'.

Globalism and regionalism

In the nineteenth century Britain was the world's leading industrial and military power. That position was challenged in the early part of the twentieth century by the rise of Germany. Germany's defeat in the First World War was only possible because of the involvement of the United States of America, but after the war the United States withdrew into isolation from European affairs, so Britain continued to play the role of the leading world power by default.

So long as Britain remained the world's leading economic power it had a vested interest in the maintenance of a world order of free trade. As British manufacturing industry was more advanced than manufacturing industry elsewhere in the world, it could expect to dominate markets that were open to trade with the world. The less developed states were more attracted to protectionism, to allow them to develop their own industrial capacity behind artificial barriers to international competition. Britain consistently condemned and resisted national protectionism.

After the Second World War it was clear that Britain was no longer the dominant industrial power in the world. The United States now occupied that position. However, the position of Britain as both an industrial and political force in the world looked to be considerably stronger than that of any capitalist state other than the United States. It was in this context that a special relationship developed between Britain and the United States. Although there was not a complete meeting of minds, there was general agreement on the desirability of an open world trading order. The United States took this as far as insisting that the preferential trading relationship that Britain enjoyed with its colonies should be ended, which caused some minor friction. Essentially, though, the traditional 'globalist' orientation of the British ruling elite was continued into the post-war era, and was taken up enthusiastically by the United States.

On political and military issues too, Britain continued to think in global terms, seeing itself as a world power with global responsibilities. This orientation was summed up by Winston Churchill in the idea of Britain standing at the centre of three overlapping spheres of influence: the Atlantic relationship, the British Empire and Commonwealth, and Europe. This doctrine, with perhaps some variation in the relative weight placed on the various elements, became part of the British post-war consensus on policy, being adopted by the Labour Foreign Secretary Ernest Bevin as well as by his Conservative successor Anthony Eden (Shlaim, Jones, and Sainsbury, 1977). Nor was it a view that was totally at variance with reality: as a legacy of its previous dominant position in the world, and of its imperial past, Britain did retain more widely ranging responsibilities than other European states. British makers of policy also retained a habit of mind that involved thinking in terms of the management of the whole global system, rather than in terms simply of narrowly defined national self-interest.

In the rest of Europe the global habit had never developed to the same extent, because no continental European power had ever succeeded in attaining the hegemonic status that Britain had. Also, the greater devastation that the war had wrought on the economies of all the continental states made their policy-makers more aware of their weakness, and necessarily more concerned with national reconstruction and security than with global order.

French concern with national reconstruction and security led to the development of regionalist tendencies. Even while the war was still being fought, schemes were being generated by advisers to the Free French leader, General de Gaulle, for West European economic groupings. The need for a wider market for French industry, if it were to operate on a scale that would allow it to compete with US industry, was realized early, even before the liberation of France. But the other reason for these schemes was to solve the German problem. After three invasions in 70 years, French analysts were only too aware that unless the threat of war between France and Germany were removed, there could be no security and no prosperity for post-war France. The focus of French thinking was therefore very different from that of British policy-makers (Young, 1984).

Combined with this, and arising out of the analysis that French technocrats made of the problems facing post-war France, there was a greater willingness on the part of French politicians to consider schemes for European reconstruction that involved some surrender of national sovereignty.

The Labour Governments, 1945—51

In the immediate post-war years the British Government seemed to hope that it might be possible to continue with the tripartite management of world affairs that had emerged in the later years of the war, with co-operation between Britain, the United States, and the Soviet Union. When it became obvious in the course of 1947 that the Soviet Union was not going to co-operate, and that Stalin was intent on establishing a stranglehold over the states of Eastern Europe, British policy came to concentrate on limiting Soviet expansionism. This objective involved ensuring that the United States did not return to isolation as it had after the First World War, and also building a West European alliance based on an Anglo-French partnership.

However, as early as 1945 proposals were emanating from Paris for a European economic union. These were discussed in July 1945 by the Foreign Office, the Treasury, and the Board of Trade. The two economic departments were opposed to such an arrangement because they believed that it would upset economic links with the Commonwealth; they also argued that the United States would be offended if a regional grouping were put before a global, multilateral trading order. 'Thus, America and the Commonwealth were judged to be more vital than Europe to British economic considerations.' (Young, 1984, pp. 37–41).

The Foreign Office was more sympathetic to the idea of an economic union, on the grounds that such a union would strengthen Western Europe politically. Indeed, until 1947 the Foreign Office appears to have advocated the creation of a West European grouping that could deal with the United States and the Soviet Union on a more equal footing than could Britain alone. Such ideas found some echoes within the Labour Party, and Ernest Bevin, the Foreign Secretary, appears to have had some sympathy with the view. But the hardening of Soviet attitudes in the course of 1947 led to a reappraisal of policy, with Bevin adopting a more Churchillian position (Shlaim, Jones, and Sainsbury, 1977, p. 42). Nevertheless, the Foreign Office continued to be sympathetic to ideas for West European economic groupings, seeing in such moves the construction of a bulwark against the spread of communism. In this it was only echoing the position of the United States – ironically so, since the risk of offending US sensibilities was one of the reasons given by the economic ministries for opposing ideas for economic unity.

At a political level, the Labour Government was prepared to accept that the economic strengthening of Western Europe was necessary as part of the defence against communism, but at no stage were Labour's leaders keen on the idea of supranationalism. Any idea that Britain might have to surrender some of its sovereignty was anathema to them. Unlike the position in continental Europe, where the idea of national sovereignty had been undermined along with the ideology of nationalism, there was still pride in the British constitution.

Here was one basis for Anglo-French disagreements over the future of Europe: the British wanted to take the lead in constructing a post-war Western Europe in which there was no place for supranationalism, while the French, prior to the return to office of de Gaulle, continually produced plans that involved supranationalism.

The Schuman Plan

The Schuman Plan was viewed as just another example of such supranationalism, and British rejection of the invitation to participate in the negotiations was ensured by the French government's demand that all participants should commit themselves in advance to accepting the principle of supranationalism. Monnet was very concerned that the British should not be allowed to enter the talks with a reserved position on this issue, because he had seen how they had already turned the Council of Europe into an intergovernmental body (Young, 1984, pp. 155–7).

Bureaucratic reactions in Britain were again marked by a divergence between the economic ministries and the Foreign Office. The economic ministries took the view that membership would risk damage to the British steel industry, and would upset the search for a global, multilateral approach to economic problems. The Foreign Office welcomed the move to re-integrate Germany in the Western system, but feared that the European grouping that might emerge could turn out to be neutralist and 'third-force' if Britain were not a member. For that reason the Foreign Office position-paper suggested that Britain ought to consider making some economic sacrifice in order to join and prevent such a turn of events (Young, 1984, p. 152).

Politically the response of the Labour Government was immediately hostile. Bevin, the Foreign Secretary, 'sensed instinctively that the Schuman Plan raised again the spectre of federalism, rather than the gradualist, functionalist method favoured by Britain'; and Stafford Cripps, the Chancellor of the Exchequer, 'deplored the plan as a move away from the idea of the Atlantic community and towards that of European Federation' (Morgan, 1984, p. 419).

To make instinctive suspicions worse, the French announcement had been made without Britain receiving any prior warning. But Dean Acheson, the US Secretary of State, had been told about it by Schuman during a visit to Paris a few days earlier, after which he had visited London and spoken to Bevin without saying anything about the scheme. Bevin, who was ill at the time and therefore perhaps more than usually irascible, immediately detected a Franco-American plot. He was somewhat mollified by explanations from Acheson and Schuman. Acheson explained that the US had had no part in hatching the plan, and that he had been sworn to secrecy by Schuman, so that he could not have told Bevin without breaking a confidence. Schuman explained the need for secrecy if the plan were not to be sabotaged by domestic French politics even before it was announced. In fact, it had not even been discussed by the French Cabinet. Also, Schuman pointed out that in September 1949 the British Government had devalued the pound by a considerable margin, from \$4 to \$2.8, without prior consultation with the French, whose own exports had been directly affected (Young, 1984, p. 150). Nevertheless, the circumstances of the announcement were far from conducive to a favourable British response.

Despite this, the British Government did not immediately reject the offer of involvement, instead setting up an *ad hoc* group of civil servants to study the implications. However, this study was overtaken by the outbreak of the Korean war, after which 'the Attlee government was preoccupied with what it saw as a far more urgent and (at that time) important and dangerous

problem than the plan for a European coal and steel industry'
(Barker 1983 p. 203).

Barker saw the British failure to participate in the Schuman
Plan as 'a turning point in Britain's post-war relations with
Western Europe'; it was the first successful post-war French
initiative taken 'without Britain and even in a sense against
Britain' (Barker 1971, p. 87).

The Pleven Plan

Franco-British relations were not improved by the episode
of the EDC. When the Korean war broke out Britain and
France had just come to agreement that the problem of German
defence should be handled by the creation of an armed police
force in West Germany, to parallel the armed militia that had
been created by the Soviet Union in East Germany. When
the US demanded the creation of a German army as a condition of sending any more troops to Western Europe, Britain
initially joined France in rejecting the demand, but Bevin quickly
gave way to US pressure and abandoned the 'police force'
scheme. France saw this as a betrayal, and a clear indication
of Britain's greater attachment to the United States (Young,
1984, pp. 167–72).

It was during the negotiations on EDC that the Conservatives
returned to office in Britain. Frequently repeated statements in
support of European unity by Winston Churchill, while he was
leader of the Opposition, had created the impression that a
change of government would produce a change in British
policy. The most recent of these statements had been to the
Assembly of the Council of Europe in August 1950, when
Churchill had said:

> Not only should we re-affirm, as we have been asked to do, our
> allegiance to the United Nations, but we should make a gesture
> of practical and constructive guidance by declaring ourselves in
> favour of the immediate creation of a European army under a
> unified command, and in which we should bear a worthy and
> honourable part. (Eden, 1960, p. 30)

Yet when the Conservatives did return to office they soon disappointed all hopes that might have been held of them. Anthony Eden, the Foreign Secretary, attending a NATO Council meeting in Rome told a press conference on 28 November 1951 that British units would not participate in the EDC. Ironically, on the same day Sir David Maxwell Fyfe, the Home Secretary and a well known pro-European, was telling the Assembly of the Council of Europe that Her Majesty's Government welcomed 'this imaginative plan'. Maxwell Fyfe (later Lord Kilmuir) was subsequently to attack Eden's statement as 'the single act which above all others destroyed Britain's name on the continent' (Sampson, 1967, p. 90). However, his own statement to the Council of Europe was seen by federalists such as the Belgian statesman Paul-Henri Spaak, as signalling British unwillingness to see the Council develop into anything beyond an inter-governmental organization. For Spaak it was a turning point in his thinking on Europe: from then he abandoned all hope of Britain leading the way, and rallied fully to the gradualist strategy of Monnet (Spaak, 1971, pp. 219–22).

Why was there this apparent change of heart by the Conservatives? Probably the answer is that the statements of support for European unity were very much a personal commitment on the part of Churchill, who as leader of the Opposition was not responsible for implementing the policy options that his rhetoric suggested. Once in office as Prime Minister, Churchill was faced with having to preside over a Cabinet in which there was by no means a majority in favour of his vision, and the resistance to it was led by the immensely influential figure of Eden, second only to Churchill himself in terms of his prestige in the Conservative Party and in the country, and by Lord Salisbury, an important figure in the pro-Empire section of the Party.

There was also opposition to the EDC from civil servants. Of all the moves for European unity the one that found least favour in Whitehall was the Pleven Plan. The implication that, if Britain joined, it would have to merge its armed forces into a European army was too alarming a surrender of national sovereignty even for the Foreign Office to contemplate. Indeed, there was a confident expectation that the plan would not succeed, because it would be too much of a surrender of sovereignty for the other potential participant states to accept. The same assessment was later to be made, incorrectly, of the Messina negotiations that resulted in the EEC; but over EDC the Foreign Office got it right.

So confident was Eden that the Pleven Plan would fail, that he had already worked out an alternative together with his officials. The frequently-repeated story that the idea for WEU came to Eden in his bath is appealing, but inaccurate. The scheme seems to have been the brainchild of Christopher Steel, an official at the Foreign Office (Carlton, 1981, p. 361). It involved extending the Brussels Treaty of 1948, a defensive Treaty between Britain, France, and the Benelux states which was designed to reconcile France in particular to the creation of a new German state. Under the British plan, the Federal Republic of Germany, and Italy, would be invited to join the signatories of the Brussels Treaty in WEU; all members except Britain would submit to WEU verification of their agreed commitments and force levels; and West Germany would in addition enter NATO on the basis of full sovereignty. This plan was accepted, albeit reluctantly in France; British inter-governmentalism seemed to have scored a significant victory over continental federalism.

The Messina negotiations

Whereas the view of British officials that the EDC would fail was proved correct, the equally confident assessment that nothing would come of the Messina negotiations proved to be completely wrong. Perhaps the farce of the Pleven Plan coloured the assessment. Whatever the reason, few voices were raised in support of Britain taking the proceedings in Italy seriously, let alone participating in the planned new Communities.

Harold Macmillan, the Chancellor of the Exchequer, wrote to Sir Edward Bridges, the senior civil servant at the Treasury, expressing his concern that Britain was being too complacent. Messina might come to nothing, but if it did prove fruitful,

Macmillan 'did not like the prospect of a world divided into the Russian sphere, the American sphere and a united Europe of which we were not a member' (Macmillan 1971, p. 74).

This advice was not heeded. Nor was the view of the United States. After a visit to Washington in February 1956, Eden, who had now succeeded Churchill as Prime Minister, and Selwyn Lloyd, the new Foreign Secretary, reported that opinion in the US Administration was enthusiastic about Messina. But even Macmillan, who was himself inclined to take the negotiations seriously, felt that the US was being naive. He thought the Americans were overlooking the risk that a high-tariff, inward-looking group would be created in Europe; that they underestimated the difficulties that participation in such an experiment would cause for Britain; and that US hostility to the idea of the Commonwealth may have been partly behind their urging Britain to take a step that would put that organization under considerable strain (Macmillan, 1971, pp. 74–5).

Initially the British Government did send a representative to the Messina negotiations, although they appear to have underestimated the importance that the other states attached to the talks, because they sent a civil servant, whereas the others sent senior political figures. Russell Bretherton, the civil servant concerned, has recorded that he was 'a little startled' on arriving at the first session to find Spaak personally presiding, and the Federal Republic of Germany represented by Walter Hallstein, the Foreign Minister (Charlton, 1983, p. 177).

British participation did not last long. After a summer recess the delegations reassembled in Brussels, when Bretherton read out a statement from the Government saying that Britain could not participate in the common market that was being proposed. After that he withdrew.

This was possibly the biggest tactical mistake that Britain made in its attempt to create the sort of Europe that it preferred. The desired form of that Europe became apparent at this time, and it was to remain very much the goal that successive British governments were to pursue thereafter. Politically it was a Europe of sovereign states, which would act together as a loyal ally of the United States. Economically it meant a Europe that would constitute a free-trade area without interventionist central policies, and open to commerce with the rest of the world. Already under Labour the broad lines of this conception of Europe had been apparent, and it was confirmed when the Conservative Government launched an independent and rival initiative to that of the Six, for a European free trade area.

Before this, in December 1955, the British Government tried to sabotage the continuing Messina negotiations by attacking the process in the OEEC. It was clear that at this stage the British saw OEEC as a preferable forum for co-operation, and they argued that the new exercise threatened its viability. Again this was a tactical error, because the intervention 'outraged Spaak and Beyen' (Burgess and Edwards, 1988, p. 411), and possibly contributed to the determination of the Six to reach agreement despite all the considerable difficulties that they were facing.

The British also attempted to enlist the help of the United States in undermining the exercise, but with a conspicuous lack of success. Early in 1956 Eden and Selwyn Lloyd visited Washington for a meeting with President Eisenhower and his Secretary of State, John Foster Dulles. They were told that the Administration considered Britain was 'ill advisedly' hostile to developments in Europe. Richard Neustadt, a historian who had privileged access to the relevant papers, stated that the US not only wanted Britain to go in, but wanted Britain 'to go in there and dominate it on behalf of joint British-American concerns' (Charlton, 1983, p. 213).

In many ways this is exactly what the new Conservative Government of Harold Macmillan decided to do in 1961 when it made the first British application for entry to the Communities of which it could have been a founder member.

The first British application

Several reasons have been suggested for the British change of heart in applying for membership of the EC in 1961: the Suez crisis in 1956, the change of Prime Minister, Britain's economic problems, the South African crisis of 1961. All of these may have played some part in the decision, but it is probably most accurate to view it as a change of tactics in pursuit of the same strategic ends, in the light of changed circumstances.

The Suez crisis certainly played some part. It has been argued that it demonstrated both the flimsiness of the special relationship with the United States, and that Britain could not rely on the Commonwealth for support in a crisis (Bailey, 1983, p. 17). It certainly led to a national reassessment of Britain's position in the world. It also led to a change of Prime Minister, with the resignation of Eden, whose instincts were consistently hostile to the idea of British participation in any form of European union, and his replacement by Macmillan, who was much more pragmatic on the issue and was even thought of as being something of a 'pro-European' within the Government.

Another consequence of Suez was a further cooling in Anglo-French relations. The French had badly wanted the removal of the Egyptian leader Colonel Nasser, whom they blamed for fomenting unrest in Algeria, and they felt that this objective at least could have been attained had Britain not called off the expedition at the first sign of pressure from the United States (Barker, 1971, p. 134). Just as over the US demand for the reconstitution of a German army in 1951, the French felt that the British Government had shown that its primary loyalty was to the United States, and not to France. This cooling of relations adversely affected the negotiations over the European free trade area, which were already going badly, and contributed to their collapse at the end of 1958. Although the European Free Trade Association (EFTA) was created at the start of the 1960s, it was without the participation of the Six. Taken in conjunction with the success of the Messina negotiations and the signing of the Treaties of Rome in 1957, this development changed the whole balance of diplomatic and economic relationships within Western Europe, creating an inner core from which Britain was excluded.

That reality seems to have been the most important consideration in the British reassessment of policy. A committee of senior civil servants which studied British relations with the Six

in 1960 concluded that 'on political grounds – that is, to ensure
a politically cohesive Western Europe – there was a strong
argument for joining the Common Market. The economic
argument was seen as less important. . .' (Barker, 1971, p. 168;
Camps, 1964, p. 293). US policy reinforced this tendency:
proposals from Britain to turn the OEEC into a close Atlantic
economic organization were rejected, and the US Administration made much of its support for the EC. The feeling
began to grow in Britain that the 'special relationship' might be
supplanted by a special relationship between the Six and the
US (Camps, 1964, p. 283).

The political considerations were given a new twist and
added saliency by the activities of the new French President,
Charles de Gaulle, who made no secret of his hostility to US
domination over Western Europe, nor of his ambition to re-
establish an independent French foreign policy. When de Gaulle
launched his plan for political co-operation in May 1960 it
became evident that his ambitions involved using the EC as the
base for such an independent French policy, a prospect that
alarmed both Britain and the United States.

The need to prevent the European grouping from developing
in a neutralist and 'third-force' direction was pressed on the
Prime Minister by the new US Administration of John F.
Kennedy. During a visit to Washington in April 1961, Macmillan
was told by Kennedy that the United States was very supportive
of British membership:

> Kennedy fully understood the economic difficulties British entry
> would bring to the United States. But these were in his mind
> overborne by the political benefits. If Britain joined the Market,
> London could offset the eccentricities of policy in Paris and
> Bonn; moreover, Britain, with its world obligations, could keep
> the EEC from becoming a high-tariff, inward-looking, white
> man's club. Above all, with British membership, the Market
> could become the basis for a true political federation of Europe.
> (Schlesinger, 1965, p. 720)

Although the thought of British sovereignty being swallowed
in a 'true political federation of Europe' may not have been

appealing to Macmillan, he does seem to have come away from Washington in no doubt that 'far from straining Anglo-American relations, Britain's joining the Community might well lead to much closer and more far-reaching transatlantic links than the British could hope to achieve in other ways', and indeed that 'the shortest, and perhaps the only, way to a real Atlantic partnership lay through Britain's joining' (Camps, 1964, p. 336).

These, then, were the primary British concerns: to prevent the EC falling under the domination of de Gaulle and turning into a regionalist grouping that did not play a full part economically or politically in the global capitalist world order; to ensure that Britain remained the leading partner of the United States in Western Europe; and to add to British influence in the world. Economic considerations came a poor fourth.

It was not even clear how far Britain, with its very different pattern of world trade, would benefit economically from membership. Whereas the original Six already conducted most of their trade with each other before membership, Britain had more trade outside than within Europe, much of it with the Commonwealth, with which she still did more trade than with the whole of Western Europe right through until 1962 (Porter, 1983, p. 128). In fact the Commonwealth was the biggest problem that the Government had to deal with in launching its bid for membership. British determination to obtain terms that were favourable to the Commonwealth delayed progress in the negotiations with the Six, which were still by no means resolved when de Gaulle imposed his veto in January 1963.

The second British application

In Opposition, the Labour Party was extremely critical of Conservative attempts to join the EC, and in their manifesto for the 1964 general election Labour was cool towards membership. But by the time of the next election, less than two years later in 1966, the tone of the Labour manifesto had changed, and after winning an increased majority in that election the new Wilson Government proceeded to revive the British application for membership.

Undoubtedly many of the same factors influenced this change of heart as had influenced the Macmillan change. The realities of government are much the same whichever party holds office. This time the economic considerations may have played a larger role. The 1964 Government had to deal with a serious balance of payments crisis, which may have undermined its confidence that the underlying health of the British economy was sufficient to allow a revival outside of any larger grouping. The EFTA experiment was not proving a success, because the organization was too imbalanced, with the large British economy clearly outweighing the economies of the other members (Austria, Denmark, Norway, Portugal, Sweden, and Switzerland). The Commonwealth states were by this time increasingly turning elsewhere for their trade: Australia and New Zealand to the United States and Japan; the African states to the EC itself. The Kennedy Round of negotiations on universal tariff reductions within the General Agreement on Tariffs and Trade (GATT) had proved to be a disappointment by 1965, while the Six were having unexpected success with their internal tariff reductions, which also involved erecting a common external tariff against the rest of the world, including Britain. Also, the difficulties being experienced by the aircraft and computer industries, two of the new technological industries which the Wilson Governments had pledged to promote, gave a clear indication that a larger domestic market was needed as a base if such industries were to be able to compete with the Americans.

Added to these economic factors were the same political considerations that had influenced Macmillan, but heightened by the changing circumstances in which British policy was being made. The questioning of Britain's role in the world, which had begun in the aftermath of Suez, had continued and the Labour Party had no satisfactory answer. In addition, the replacement of Kennedy by Lyndon Johnson as President marked a shift from a cosmopolitan US Administration, which was at least receptive to European (including British) concerns, to a more domestically oriented Administration. Growing British concern about aspects of US policy, particularly in Vietnam but also over the invasion of the Dominican Republic in 1965, brought Britain closer to de Gaulle's France in its attitude to the global political order. Perhaps unswerving support for the United States was not the best way to promote world order after all.

Despite all these signs of movement away from Atlanticism towards Europeanism in the British position, de Gaulle blocked the second application on the same grounds as he had the first. He still believed that Britain was too wedded to the United States. Britain's membership therefore had to await the departure of de Gaulle from office, which came in May 1969 when he resigned following defeat in a national referendum.

Britain's entry to the EC

Events moved rapidly after the resignation of de Gaulle. At a meeting of the Council of Ministers in July 1969 the Commission was asked to prepare an updated version of its opinion on enlargement which had first been submitted in September 1967. This was ready by October, and was favourable to enlargement. Maurice Schumann, the French Foreign Minister, indicated that France would not renew its veto, provided that the transitional period of the EC was first completed by finalizing arrangements for financing the common agricultural policy; and that the Six agreed, in advance of opening negotiations with Britain, on how the Community could be further developed and strengthened.

The Labour Government had left its original application on the table, and was prepared to begin negotiations as soon as the Six were ready; but before they were, the June 1970 general election produced a Conservative Government, which immediately pursued the application as one of its top priorities. Anthony Barber was appointed as Heath's chief negotiator (although he was soon to became Chancellor of the Exchequer, following the death of Iain Macleod, to be replaced as chief negotiator by Geoffrey Rippon), and negotiations opened on

30 June 1970, in Luxembourg.

In his opening statement Barber highlighted a problem that was to dog Britain's relations with the EC for most of the next fifteen years: the effect of the newly negotiated financing arrangements on Britain's potential net contributions to the Community's budget. The Labour Government had hoped to take part in the negotiation of the new arrangements, but had not been invited. In 1967 the Commission had said that the existing arrangements, if applied to Britain, would give rise to a problem, and the new arrangements had made that potential problem even more severe (Barker, 1971, p. 247).

Nevertheless, the Government negotiated seriously to obtain membership. Heath's strategy was to get into the Community as quickly as possible, and then solve any difficulties that remained, from inside (Young, 1973, p. 211). When the negotiations got bogged down, Heath held a personal meeting with Georges Pompidou, de Gaulle's successor, which broke through the logjam (Kitzinger, 1973, pp. 119–25). Indeed, in the course of 1971–2 extensive bilateral Anglo-French discussions took place, without which success in the formal negotiations might not have been achieved (Wallace, 1984, p. 23). As it was, agreement was reached on the terms of British entry after eighteen months of negotiations, a treaty was signed in Brussels in January 1972, and Britain became a member of the EC on 1 January 1973.

The Heath Government

Edward Heath's personal commitment to the ideal of European unity was never in doubt. It is largely on the basis of that personal commitment that the Heath Government retains the reputation of having been the most pro-EC British government; but no single person, not even the Prime Minister, is the sole fount of policy, and even during the Heath years the broad parameters of the policy of the British State to the EC did not change dramatically.

The participation of the British Government in the work of

the EC began before formal membership on 1 January 1973. In October 1972 a summit meeting was held in Paris of the Heads of Government of the enlarged Community, which mapped out areas of priority for future action. Heath's influence helped to put three items into the final communiqué. One was the priority given to negotiating a European Regional Development Fund. It was through such a mechanism that Heath hoped to solve the potential problem of Britain's net contributions to the budget: by creating a fund from which Britain could benefit. The second item was a common policy for energy, an issue about which Heath felt strong concern in the light of the instability of the Middle East, which supplied most of Europe's oil. The third item was agreement to pursue a joint approach to trade talks with the United States in the context of GATT.

On this last issue, Heath wanted the EC to take a hard line in insisting that an early date be fixed for the start of the talks, and that the issue of non-tariff barriers to trade be placed on the agenda. In this he was in harmony with President Pompidou. Because Heath and Pompidou often found themselves in agreement on the necessity of Europe taking a joint stand against the United States on commercial questions, it is easy to form the impression that Heath was departing from traditional British positions in international affairs. Undeniably he was departing from the usual closeness of Britain to the United States on economic questions; but it was the United States that had departed from the normal Anglo-American position, while the Heath Government remained loyal to that position.

In 1971 President Nixon had ended the convertibility of the dollar into gold, thereby bringing to an end the Bretton Woods system of fixed exchange rates. At the same time he had imposed a 10 per cent surcharge on those imports into the United States that were already subject to duties, which amounted to about 50 per cent of all US imports, and introduced a freeze on wage and price increases, to tackle the growing problem of domestic inflation (Morse, 1973, pp. 253–5).

These measures, which were taken unilaterally, marked a turning away of the United States from its consistent post-war defence of multilateral free trade, and inaugurated a period when US economic policy was conducted with an eye more on the domestic economic and political consequences than on the consequences for the international system. As well as the tariff increases, the US Administration adopted or tolerated the introduction of a whole range of non-tariff barriers to free trade, all designed to reserve the domestic market for domestic producers in the face of rising international competition. It was against these departures from the established Anglo-American policies on economic management that the Heath Government attempted to organize the EC, with the support of the French President, who may well have had somewhat different motives.

In other respects also the attitude of the British at Paris remained consistent with that displayed by successive governments prior to membership. Heath stood out against common policies in the areas of industry, science, and technology; and against a common social policy. Interventionist common policies were no more welcome to the Heath Government than they were to its predecessors or successors. The exception, the British campaign for a European regional fund, tends to obscure this perception; but the regional fund was seen purely as a pragmatic response to the need to balance the common agricultural policy in a way that would benefit Britain. It was based on an acceptance that the agricultural policy was not going to be changed, and that therefore the only way of preventing Britain from being a major net contributor to the budget was to call into existence this balancing item of expenditure. Nor did the pursuit of a common regional fund imply support for an interventionist EC regional policy: what the British Government was looking for was a subsidy for its existing regional development policy.

Despite British opposition, common industrial and social policies were included in the communiqué of the Paris summit; but pride of place went to the aim of achieving economic and monetary union by the end of 1981. British acceptance of this objective does appear to mark rather a large step away from the policy of previous governments of trying to limit the EC to being a free-trade area. However, the acceptance of the objective has to be seen in its context. Economic and monetary union was one of the three objectives agreed at The Hague in 1969, and was linked to the enlargement negotiations: it was therefore rather difficult for the British to oppose it. French and German agreement to the key British objective of a regional development fund was probably linked to British acceptance of economic and monetary union. There was considerable dispute between France and Germany on how to progress towards economic and monetary union, which left open the prospect of Britain being able to prevent any serious erosion of sovereign powers over economic management. Also, the chaos that was threatening the world monetary system in the aftermath of Nixon's 1971 bombshell, and the apparent indifference of the United States to the effects of this on the rest of the world, made the monetary union aspect not unwelcome to Britain as a means of restoring some order to the system.

Even when all these factors are borne in mind, there does seem to have been some difference of opinion within the British Government on the advisability of economic and monetary union. Although the pound joined the 'snake in the tunnel' in March 1972, it was withdrawn in the face of speculative pressure in July, and the Treasury refused to put it back in unless the German Government would fully underwrite its agreed value (Tsoukalis, 1977, p. 128). This was precisely the sort of commitment that the Germans were refusing to make to the other member states without prior agreement on the co-ordination of domestic economic policies, and was therefore a demand which the Treasury could hardly have expected would be met.

At the same time as refusing to assist progress to monetary union, Britain continued to insist on the necessity of the regional development fund, thereby breaking what to the Germans appeared to be a tacit deal. Matters became worse after the outbreak of the 1973 Arab-Israeli war disrupted supplies of oil from the Middle East to Europe.

Heath had been insisting since before the Paris summit on the necessity for the EC to develop a common policy on energy, but by this he meant a common stance towards the oil-producing states. This was part of his concern to use the EC as a substitute for US leadership in management of the international system. After the 1973 disruption to oil supplies, Heath renewed his demand for such a policy, but the other member states, led by France, insisted that any such move should be accompanied by agreements on an internal policy involving agreement to pool energy resources in a time of crisis. This was unacceptable to Britain, which was on the verge of becoming an oil producer itself. To retain control over this national asset was an important practical and political objective of the British Government, as well as being consistent with the long-standing British reluctance to surrender sovereignty in general to the EC.

It was the dispute over oil sharing that finally caused the collapse of Heath's hopes for a substantial regional development fund. The energy question so soured relations with Germany that no agreement had been reached on the size of the fund, before the fall of the Heath Government in the 1974 general election.

Although the Heath Government showed more sympathy with the idea of European unity than any of either its predecessors or successors, its support owed much to the special circumstances of the time, in which the United States had abandoned responsibility for management of the international system. Heath attempted to fill that gap by organizing the EC as a strong actor in world affairs under British leadership, much as de Gaulle had tried to organize it under French leadership. The objectives that the British Government was pursuing were no different from those of its predecessors: the defence of a multilateral free-trading world order, and the maintenance of stability in the capitalist system. Just as Britain's application for membership of the EC was less a change of direction than a change of tactics, so the Heath Government's strong support for EC unity was an adaptation of the established policy of the British State to changed international circumstances.

The Wilson and Callaghan Governments

The policy of the British State towards European integration has been coloured predominantly by the objective of ensuring that Western Europe does not become an inward-looking regional grouping; but since 1973 it has also been concerned with minimizing the economic costs of British membership of the EC. Another aspect, which is dealt with in the next chapter, and which has overlain these predominant objectives, has concerned domestic political considerations.

During the Wilson Governments of 1974–6, the first of these objectives was less dominant than in any other period; the objective of minimizing the economic costs of membership was apparent; but the domestic political considerations were uppermost. This was a period when the country was fundamentally divided in the aftermath of the failure of Heath's attempts to curb the power of the trade unions, and his effective defeat by the miners in the strike of 1974. Rising inflation and unemployment, consequences in part of the December 1973 rise in the price of oil, added to the sense of crisis. In this context, Wilson successfully used the issue of the terms of British entry to the EC to divert attention from the economic crisis and social tensions. He also used it as a means of outmanoeuvring the left within the Labour Party and reasserting his authority. This story, the story of the renegotiation of the terms of entry and the referendum, is told in the next chapter.

International considerations were very much secondary to domestic preoccupations in determining the policies that Wilson followed. They did figure prominently, though, in the policies of his successor, James Callaghan. During the period of Callaghan's premiership the differences grew wider, between the United States on the one hand and France and Germany on the other, over the management of the international system. French President Valéry Giscard d'Estaing had initiated a programme of economic summits of the major capitalist states in November 1975, and these continued to function as a forum for the co-ordination of policy; but the German Chancellor, Helmut Schmidt, found it increasingly difficult to accept that the new US Administration of Jimmy Carter was exercising responsible leadership. In these circumstances the Franco-German inclination was to move ahead to adopt European solutions, particularly to monetary problems, whereas the British Government returned to its pre-Heath, pre-Nixon role of advocate of Atlantic co-operation, and mediator between the EC and the United States.

It was in the role of mediator that in March 1978 Callaghan launched a plan to float the capitalist world out of recession in a 'convoy'. This was in response to the German rejection of Carter's own plan for the strong capitalist economies to act as a 'locomotive', which would pull the weaker economies out of recession. Callaghan's alternative involved co-ordinated policy responses to achieve a simultaneous stimulus to the world economy from the states with low inflation, and measures of monetary restraint in those with high rates of inflation. It was an initiative that actually produced concrete agreements at the Bonn economic summit in July 1978, and could have achieved a degree of success had its effects not been distorted by the renewed chaos introduced into the international economic system by the Iranian revolution and the consequent second round of steep increases in the price of oil.

Before this stage was reached, the French President and the German Chancellor had unveiled their own plan for a new advance towards economic and monetary union, the EMS. Although presented by both Giscard and Schmidt as part of a 'phased march' towards a new world system, rather than an attempt to create an exclusive regional monetary system (McKinlay and Little, 1986, p. 163), both Callaghan and Carter were concerned at the possible implications, preferring to tackle international monetary problems through existing institutions such as the International Monetary Fund (Statler, 1979, p. 215; Garavaglio, 1984, p. 19).

So, although domestic political considerations figured in Callaghan's decision not to take sterling fully into the EMS, the familiar British concern about regionalism was also a significant factor. The most significant consideration, though, was probably the anticipated effects on the British economy, which several expert studies predicted would be damaging (Statler, 1979, p. 223; Gardner, 1987, pp. 120–3). In fact it seems possible that Callaghan only went along with the setting up of the EMS at all because of an understanding reached at the Bremen meeting of the European Council in July 1978 that progress on the EMS would be accompanied by a re-examination of Britain's contributions to the budget of the EC (Hornsby, 1978).

This long-standing problem came to the fore again in the course of 1978, as Britain approached the end of its transitional period of membership, and so the time when it would have to pay its full contribution. It rapidly became clear that the formula, which had been agreed as part of the renegotiation package, for correcting the imbalance in British net contributions compared to Britain's relative wealth, was going to prove ineffective. In 1979 Britain, with the third lowest *per capita* gross domestic product in the EC, would become the second largest net contributor to the budget. This was a major problem that the Callaghan Government bequeathed to its Conservative successor.

The Thatcher Governments

Margaret Thatcher's Governments after 1979 continued with much the same policies towards the EC as previous British governments. From 1979 to mid-1984 the emphasis was on correcting the imbalance in Britain's contributions to the budget. After the Fontainebleau meeting of the European Council in June 1984 a new agenda emerged around the idea of freeing the internal market of the EC by the end of 1992, an idea that was supported enthusiastically by the British Government, although it was less enthusiastic about other parts of the 1992 programme that other member states saw as essential complements to the freeing of the market.

Mrs Thatcher took an extremely determined and even confrontational approach to the negotiations on British budgetary contributions. She upset her partners by repeatedly refusing

what they considered to be reasonable offers for rebates, and
by linking the issue to reform of the common agricultural policy,
a sacred cow of the original member states which they would
not abandon easily because of the domestic political influence
of the farmers. The reasons for the nationalistic tone in which
Thatcher conducted her part of the negotiations are considered
in the next chapter, where they are treated as a reflection of
domestic political circumstances. But in the demand for reform of the common agricultural policy the normal policy of
the British State can be detected.

British insistence on reform of the agricultural policy reflected
the fact that Britain's imbalance in net contributions to the
budget was due to its relatively low level of receipts from the
agricultural funds which dominated the budget. But as well
as the objective of minimizing the economic cost to Britain
of membership of the EC, there was also the objective that
has been described above as globalism. Agriculture is the
biggest export industry of the United States; the common
agricultural policy, which gives preference to EC farmers within the Community and subsidizes their exports to the rest
of the world, has been the biggest single cause of friction
between the United States and the EC.

Eventually a settlement of the budgetary dispute was reached
at the Fontainebleau meeting of the European Council in June
1984. Although it was not an unfavourable settlement for Britain,
it was only marginally more favourable than agreements that
had been offered, and rejected, earlier. Nor did this settlement
involve a radical reform of the common agricultural policy,
although there was some progress on reform in separate negotiations. The most likely reason why the Government accepted
the settlement at this time was that the other members of the
EC, led by French President François Mitterrand, were openly
talking of proceeding with a new initiative to further European
integration, without Britain if necessary.

This possibility worried the British Government because
it opened up the prospect once again of the EC falling under
French leadership, and following a line of development that
might result in the emergence of a closed regional bloc.

Mitterrand's initiatives were openly inspired by concern that the United States and Japan were forging ahead of the EC in the new technology industries, and that the US and Japanese economies were outperforming the EC. In other words, there seemed to be a revival of Gaullist thinking (albeit from a Socialist President) on the purposes of European integration, stressing the threat to Europe from non-European competitors. To counter this threat, Mitterrand proposed a joint European programme of technological research, and a drive to free the internal market of the EC of non-tariff barriers to trade which prevented European firms operating freely across national boundaries.

For the British Government the idea of freeing the internal market of the EC was attractive because it appeared at one and the same time to serve Britain's economic interests, to coincide with Thatcher's attachment to free market economics, and to be a means of moving other member states away from their attachment to non-tariff barriers to trade that interfered with the proper functioning of the wider international capitalist system.

So far as British economic interests were concerned, the freeing of the internal market included commitments to remove barriers to free trade in financial services and in transport (particularly air transport), restrictions that were particularly damaging to the prospects of the British economy performing well within the EC, these being areas in which Britain appeared to have a comparative advantage.

So far as Thatcher's commitment to free-market economics is concerned, little more needs to be said other than the obvious point that from this perspective the freeing of the market was an end in itself, and formed the complete 1992 project. Part of the disagreement between Thatcher and other EC leaders arose because they saw the freeing of the market as only one component of the project, needing to be balanced and complemented by other measures.

The persistence of non-tariff barriers to trade throughout the capitalist world was a serious concern of the United States, which saw the EC as a major culprit in this departure from the principle of multilateral free trade. It was not coincidental that the Uruguay Round of GATT negotiations, which began in 1986, had these issues as the main items on its agenda. Here again, Britain could be seen as acting in a manner that was consistent with US views, and with defence of the global internationalism that the United States consistently advocated.

However, the removal of non-tariff barriers to trade between the members of the EC would only be welcome to the United States if accompanied or followed by a dismantling of the same non-tariff barriers relative to the rest of the world. The alternative of a 'fortress Europe' was certainly not welcome to the United States, as it made clear. Britain also fought against any suggestion that the EC should become inward-looking and even protectionist against the rest of the world after 1992.

It did not seem that other member states saw matters in quite the same way. The freeing of the internal market was certainly not an end in itself for François Mitterrand, the French President, nor for Jacques Delors, the President of the Commission, for whom 1992 appeared to have five aspects. One was the freeing of the internal market. The second was the institution of a European programme of economic and technological research, which was effected in the form of the EC's framework programmes in telecommunications, biotechnology, electronics, and the application of advanced technology; and through the EUREKA programme for European collaboration on technological research, which extends beyond the EC to involve other states of Western Europe. The third aspect was the achievement of a genuine economic and monetary union; the fourth was what came to be termed 'the social dimension'; and the fifth was reform of the decision-making procedures of the EC, to strengthen the role of the central institutions.

Each of these elements could have served to feed European regionalism. The freeing of the internal market would allow an economy to emerge that was large enough to insulate itself against the outside world if necessary, and not suffer the disadvantages that would ensue to the economy of a single state that tried to do the same thing. The programme of technological research and development was designed to keep Europe in the race with Japan and the United States to dominate the high technology markets and particularly the capital goods industries. An economic and monetary union was essential if Europe was to be economically unified internally, and not subject to having its policies driven off course by decisions taken in other parts of the world, particularly the United States. The social dimension was clearly designed to obtain the consent of trade unions to the freeing of the internal market, which at least in the short term carried with it risks to jobs; but adoption of a 'social charter' involved giving workers a degree of protection that was not available to workers in other capitalist states that competed with the EC states, and would therefore risk EC products being rendered uncompetitive; and this in turn could well be used as an excuse for excluding the free entry of goods from non-members to the post-1992 market, so that the social dimension could have become the key which locked the door of a 'fortress Europe'. Institutional reform would have weakened the ability of the British Government to block such moves towards regionalism.

In a speech in Bruges in September 1988, Thatcher attacked the extended 1992 project on a number of fronts. What received the most attention from the Press throughout Europe was her assertion that Europe would be stronger with 'France as France, Spain as Spain, Britain as Britain, each with its own customs, traditions and identities' and that 'it would be folly to try to fit them into some sort of identikit European personality' (Thatcher, 1988, p. 4). This was seen by the European media as a reassertion of nationalism in the tradition of General de Gaulle.

Yet the focus on this passage in the speech perhaps indicates that the media generally approached it expecting an assertion of nationalism, and leapt upon evidence that confirmed their expectation. In fact the passage took up only one page of the published version of the speech, which ran to nine pages. Far more frequent than assertions of British nationalism were assertions of British internationalism.

The speech began with a strong affirmation of Britain's acceptance of its European identity, reviewing the historical role of Britain in Europe, and making an unequivocal statement: 'Britain does not dream of some cosy, isolated existence on the fringes of the European Community. Our destiny is in Europe, as part of the Community' (Thatcher, 1988, p. 3). However, that statement was accompanied by an equally strong qualification: 'That is not to say that our future lies *only* in Europe.' This was a reassertion of the established British position, as was the insistence that: 'The European Community is *one* manifestation of that European identity. But it is not the only one' (Thatcher, 1988, p. 2).

The rest of the Bruges speech contained many passages that were internationalist in tone. Indeed, the last of four 'guiding principles' which Thatcher identified was 'that Europe should not be isolationist' (Thatcher, 1988, p. 7). On the other hand, as the Press showed, the Prime Minister's objections could be presented as expressions of nationalist sentiment, and to some extent were so presented by the Prime Minister herself.

Thus, the rejection of centralized control of the European economy from Brussels was apparently contrasted with national control. The passage in which she said: 'But working more closely together does *not* require power to be centralised in Brussels or decisions to be taken by an appointed bureaucracy' (Thatcher, 1988, p. 4) suggested a contrast with decisions democratically taken in national parliaments. It is equally plausible, though, to suggest that Thatcher's rejection of centralized control was based on suspicion of the purposes for which that centralized control would be used. Not only could it have implied a more interventionist and directive role in economic affairs than was acceptable to her own liberal economic philosophy, it could also have implied the closure of the EC market to open commerce with the rest of the world.

Thatcher's objections to the social dimension were again expressed in nationalist terms: not allowing a democratic choice of the British people to be overturned from Brussels: 'We have not successfully rolled back the frontiers of the state in Britain, only to see them reimposed at a European level, with a European super-state exercising a new dominance from Brussels' (Thatcher, 1988, p. 4).

Again, though, it was compatible with a desire not to see a wedge driven between Europe and the rest of the world. Her other refrain was that: 'we certainly do not need new regulations which raise the cost of *employment* and make Europe's labour market less flexible and less competitive with overseas suppliers' (Thatcher, 1988, p. 7). Proposals such as the harmonization of social security benefits, and the introduction of workers' rights to information on the investment plans of companies, were liable to render European industry uncompetitive with companies in other parts of the world that did not have to pay the taxes necessary to sustain high social benefits, did not have to bear the direct burden of paying employees during periods of pregnancy and child rearing, and did not have to reduce their flexibility by having to inform their employees of their investment plans. The fact that all European companies would have the same obligations would only make any difference if the intention was to insulate the European market from wider international competition.

So, although the Press treated the Bruges speech as a sustained assertion of nationalism, it was also compatible with the global internationalism, and resistance to European regionalism, that had been a constant of the policy of the British State towards the EC under successive governments since 1945.

Conclusion

The policy of the British State towards European integration has remained broadly consistent under successive governments. It has been marked above all by a concern to prevent an exclusive regional grouping emerging in Western Europe which would disrupt the global economic and political order that the British State consistently supported. After circumstances made British membership of the EC necessary in pursuit of this primary objective, the subsidiary objective emerged of minimizing the cost to Britain of membership.

These objectives explain in large part the positions taken

up by successive British governments towards European integration and the EC. Initially Britain supported forms of integration which were intergovernmental in nature, and which did not involve going beyond economic free trade. A serious underestimation of the commitment of the six original EC states to a closer form of integration led to Britain becoming marginalized within Western Europe, so that by the late 1950s, 'the British Government had lost the initiative and was reacting to European situations created by others; it was not itself setting the pace' (Camps, 1964, p. 505). This eventually resulted in the British applications for membership of the EC: a reversal of tactics which was made necessary by the prospect of a French-dominated regional grouping emerging.

Once membership was achieved, the subsidiary objective of minimizing the cost to Britain emerged. For the Heath Government this meant pursuing the creation of a substantial European regional development fund. For the Wilson Government it meant renegotiating the terms of entry. For the Callaghan Government it meant not taking sterling fully into the EMS, and raising once again the issue of Britain's contributions to the budget of the EC. For the Thatcher Governments it again meant the budgetary issue, which dominated the period from 1979 to 1984. This remained, however, a subsidiary objective. The primary objective was still the prevention of European regionalism.

Although the Heath Government appeared not to follow the same policy, because of the drive to achieve EC policies in opposition to those of the United States, this was again more of a tactical adjustment to circumstances than a departure from the general strategy of global internationalism. It was the Nixon Administration which abandoned the commitment to multilateral free trade; the British Government was attempting to organize the EC as a champion of those values which had hitherto been common ground between Britain and the United States.

International considerations hardly affected the policies of the Wilson Governments, which were concerned predominantly with domestic political problems; but the same general approach was evident again in the attempts of the Callaghan Government to act as a mediator between the United States and the EC.

For the Thatcher Governments the point at which the budgetary battle had to be settled was the point at which the EC threatened to move ahead again without the restraining hand of the British State on the steering wheel. Preventing a re-emergence of the threat of regionalism took priority over the objective of minimizing the costs to Britain of EC membership. Although both objectives were present in the dispute between Mrs Thatcher and the rest of the EC over the extent of the 1992 project, which dominated the late 1980s, the emphasis of the Press on the nationalism of the British Prime Minister ignored how far the objective of preventing regionalism could also be an explanation of the positions taken by Britain.

This concentration of the Press on the nationalist rhetoric of Thatcher may have been precisely what the rhetoric was designed to achieve. Ever since membership was first mooted, the tone in which the EC has been discussed by British statespersons has reflected the fact that they are also politicians who have to sustain the support of their political parties and of the electorate behind their actions in the domain of foreign policy. This dimension has been relatively ignored in the book up to now, in order to focus attention on the consistencies in the policy of the British State across all governments. In the next chapter the focus shifts to the domestic political dimension.

3 Party Politics and European Integration

Ever since the decision of the Macmillan Government to apply for membership of the EC, European integration has been an important issue in domestic British politics. At times it has become the most important single issue; and certain aspects of the attitude of British governments to the EC have been the direct result of domestic political constraints.

Electoral constraints have been important, but largely because neither of the major political parties has been prepared to give a clear and unequivocal lead to the electorate in favour of European integration. Only the minor parties of the centre (Liberals, Social Democrats) have been consistent in their support for the EC. Both the major parties have been internally divided, and as a result their leaders have generally been forced to take a line which has enabled them to hold together so far as possible the different factions in their parties.

The attitudes of party leaders to European integration, especially when their party has been in office, have largely been determined by the objectives outlined in the previous chapter; but the rhetoric of British politicians on the issue has been heavily influenced by the requirements of 'party statecraft' (Bulpitt, 1988).

Public opinion

Public opinion in Britain only slowly came round to support for membership of the EC. With the significant exception of a brief period around the time of the 1975 referendum, public opinion surveys showed only between a quarter and a third of the electorate in favour of British membership through until the middle 1980s, after which time there was a steady increase in support, culminating in a majority of 55 per cent evaluating British membership as a 'good thing' in May 1989 (Gallup Poll, 1989). A number of explanations may be offered for this reluctance to embrace membership.

Whereas in most of continental western Europe the experience of the Second World War undermined nationalism, in Britain it reinforced an already strongly developed sense of national identity. In the six original member states of the EC, politicians presented participation in the process of European integration to the electorate as an ideal which would reduce the force of nationalism and the risk of a future European war.

In Britain there was no such ideological support for integration: membership of the EC was presented to the electorate in purely pragmatic terms, as something that was necessary for the economic well-being of the country. For the British people, European integration was at best a necessity, not the realization of an ideal.

That difference of attitude was reinforced by the fact that Britain did not become a member of the EC until after the rapid economic growth of the 1960s came to an end. British membership coincided with the onset of persistent recession. Whereas the citizens of the original six member states came to identify the EC with prosperity in the early years, the population of Britain had no such positive experience.

Britain's geographical position as an island on the edge of Europe must also have contributed to the less positive view of integration. For the people of the continental heartland, European integration was more of a daily reality: businesses operated across frontiers, and people of different nationalities were in regular contact with one another. In Britain such contact was much less frequent. The rest of Europe remained 'overseas' in the perception of much of the British population, even at the end of the 1980s.

But perhaps the most significant factor was the attitude of

Britain's political leaders. Had there been a leader who was committed to the ideal of European integration, and brave enough to defy the dominant ideology of narrow nationalism in public statements, there might have been a change in the electorate. But Edward Heath was the only leader of either of the major parties who might have had the personal commitment, and even he tended to talk in much more pragmatic terms. Others, both Conservative and Labour, gave no lead in the direction of European integration, often quite the contrary.

The Conservative Party

Both the major British parties are coalitions of different political groups, which in a different political system might well exist as separate parties. The Conservative Party contains the heirs of the Tory tradition of paternalism, but also free-market liberals, and pragmatic modernizers like Edward Heath who have little time for either the concept of tradition which inspires the Tories or the dogmatic adherence to the virtues of the free market which inspires the new liberals.

Of these three groups, the traditional Tories have tended to be the strongest opponents of British membership of the EC; the liberals have been supporters of membership so long as European integration could be limited to economic integration on free-market principles; while the pragmatic modernizers have been the strongest supporters of EC membership, and even of a degree of central direction of economic policy from Brussels so far as this has been likely to contribute to the renewal and regeneration of the British economy.

No leader of the Conservative Party can afford to ignore any one of these factions completely, and the rhetoric of the leader will usually contain elements of the language used by each of the groups. This has applied to the rhetoric used in connection with European integration as much as, if not more than, it has applied to other issues.

Harold Macmillan is perhaps remembered as a traditional Tory because of his criticisms of the social and economic policies of the Thatcher Governments during his later years when (as Lord Stockton) he was a member of the House of Lords. But it is probably more accurate to see Macmillan the Prime Minister as a pragmatic modernizer. His association with the policy of British withdrawal from the Empire in Africa was in line with a concern to reduce insupportable external commitments as part of a strategy of economic modernization, and it led him into conflict with the traditional Tory wing of the Party, which saw an attachment to Empire as one of the bedrocks of Conservatism. The decision to apply for membership of the EC ran into resistance from the same quarter.

Macmillan was aided in weathering the storm by the tradition within the Conservative Party of loyalty to the leader, and by the prosperity of the country in the 1950s, which although based on a relatively poor economic performance in comparison with other West European states was nevertheless impressive by previous British standards. The prosperity meant that Macmillan was able to present himself as a successful Prime Minister, who could win further electoral success for the Conservative Party, which made unassailable his position as leader.

At the same time, even a successful Prime Minister has to hold his colleagues in the Cabinet and in the Party behind him, and so it was probably inevitable that when Macmillan came to the conclusion that Britain should apply for membership of the EC, he presented the decision to Parliament and the country in purely pragmatic terms. There was no attempt to replace the strong sense of national identity that still existed in Britain with an alternative sense of a European destiny, which had been the way in which the formation of the EC had been sold to the electorates of the original six member states. Whatever Macmillan's personal feelings about European integration, his approach of 'backing into Europe', as his critics put it, was the only prudent course available. No British Prime Minister could have expected to be taken seriously had he begun to espouse the virtues of a federal Europe to the British public at a time when nationalism formed a part of the underlying political consensus.

Both major parties had a history of nationalism. For the Conservatives suddenly to become European federalists would have been to court electoral disaster: the Labour Party would have jumped at the chance to attack its opponents for a lack of patriotism, and to accuse them of selling the nation to foreigners. Such attitudes were just as prevalent amongst many of the Tory rank-and-file.

The legacy of Macmillan's approach to the first application was that debate on the issue continued to be conducted in terms of what best served the national interest. There was no appeal to the ideals of furthering peace and overcoming nationalism which were so powerful a part of the debates on European integration on the Continent. Opponents of the EC attempted to show that membership involved costs for Britain that were not outweighed by the benefits; supporters argued that it was the other way round. There were few voices raised at any stage to say that some costs were acceptable in order to serve a higher purpose. Without that dimension to the debate, the rhetoric of politicians was always likely to sound negative.

Within the Conservative Party the doubts raised at the time of the Macmillan application were resurrected when the Heath Government pursued the application which its Labour predecessor had renewed. But these doubts were overridden by the the new Prime Minister, whose determination to enter the EC was fired by his own long-standing personal commitment and by the role that membership played in his strategy for modernizing the British economy.

Another key aspect of this strategy was the reform of the trade unions, a serious barrier to the restructuring of the economy that even the preceding Labour Government, beholden as it was to the trade unions, had been forced to recognize. In these two ways Heath's programme for revitalizing Britain bore strong resemblances to Wilson's programme. But Wilson's failure to gain entry to the EC and to push through his trade union reforms had put him on the defensive within the Labour Party and had forced him to oppose the measures which he must have known were necessary to Britain's economic future, in order to ensure his own political survival. Instead of a new consensus emerging around membership of the EC and reform of industrial relations, both became issues of controversy between the political parties (Frankel, 1975, pp. 311–12; Newman, 1983, p. 222).

The replacement of Heath by Margaret Thatcher as leader in 1975 did not change the formal commitment of the Party to membership of the EC, but there was a distinct change of tone. Thatcher from the outset made it clear that whilst recognizing the need for British membership of the EC, she would vigorously defend British national interests, and oppose supranationalism.

During the first period of the Thatcher Governments' dealings with the EC, the phase from 1979 to 1984 when the budgetary dispute dominated, nationalistic rhetoric was very much to the fore. After the settlement of the budgetary issue in mid-1984 there seemed to be a change of tone as the Government aligned itself behind the objective of freeing the internal market of the EC by the end of 1992. But the nationalistic tone reasserted itself gradually, especially in the pronouncements of the Prime Minister, culminating in her infamous Bruges speech of October 1988.

According to some commentators (for example, Peter Jenkins in his columns in *The Independent*), the nationalistic tone could be explained fully by reference to the prejudices of the Prime Minister herself. However, it is not necessary to deny that Mrs Thatcher's instincts lay in this direction to recognize that domestic political considerations were also compatible with the strong nationalist tone.

When Margaret Thatcher became leader of the Conservative Party she did so as a candidate of the right wing, a coalition of neo-liberals committed to free market economics, and Tory nationalists. Her free-market credentials were easily established, but she had to allay doubts about the strength of her nationalism. While in opposition she did this primarily by vigorous support for the British independent nuclear deterrent, linked with attacks on the Soviet Union that earned her the title of 'the iron lady'. But when she became Prime Minister in 1979, some of the measures that she took, such as the abolition of exchange controls and the freeing of capital movements, could have been presented as being against the national interest. It was therefore important for Thatcher to re-establish her nationalist credentials, both in order to counter the charge from the Labour Opposition that she was selling out the national interest, and to reassure her nationalist supporters within the Conservative Party, where her position was far from secure.

To underline her nationalism, Thatcher chose to fight the battle with the EC over Britain's budgetary contributions in a very public and confrontational manner, using phrases about wanting Britain's money back, which were anathema to the rest of the EC, but were designed primarily for domestic consumption. It should be stressed, though, that there was nothing new in either the cause or the approach. Callaghan's Government had clearly signalled its intention to contest the size of budgetary contributions as a priority matter. And the approach of battling against the EC with a Union flag metaphorically draped over one shoulder had been perfected by Harold Wilson during the renegotiation of the terms of entry. As during the Wilson period, the tone adopted was determined by domestic political considerations, and may even have been counter-productive in obtaining the terms sought within the EC.

Once that phase ended, with the Fontainebleau settlement, the Thatcher Government threw its support behind the programme to free the internal market. But the Prime Minister's statements, especially her Bruges speech (which is analysed in chapter 2 above) continued to have a decidedly nationalist tone. If, as argued above, the opposition of the Government to certain aspects of the 1992 programme can be understood as an expression of the established policy of the British State, the domestic political arena must still be judged to have influenced the tone of the Prime Minister's statements on the EC.

In the course of 1989 the internal opposition to Thatcher's approach began to build steadily. Heath's criticisms, which had begun soon after his defeat in the leadership election, could perhaps be dismissed. But to Heath's voice was joined that of Michael Heseltine, a popular figure within the Party who was seen by some as a credible future challenger for the leadership. More importantly still, it was increasingly evident that there was a split within the Cabinet itself, with such senior figures as the Foreign Secretary, Sir Geoffrey Howe, and the Chancellor of the Exchequer, Nigel Lawson, pressing for sterling to be put into the exchange rate mechanism of the EMS, a move which Thatcher was reluctant to make. Eventually, in October 1989, Lawson resigned over the issue. The shock of the resignation added to a growing feeling in senior Conservative and Government circles that the Prime Minister's approach to European matters was too negative and was not helping Britain to achieve its diplomatic objectives.

By the end of 1989 the Press detected a change in the tone of Thatcher's pronouncements on the EC. For example, at the June 1989 meeting of the European Council in Madrid, the Prime Minister for the first time laid down four specific conditions which when met would allow sterling to enter the exchange rate mechanism of the EMS, a definite advance on her previous vague formula that sterling would enter 'when the time was right'. (The conditions were that other states should remove their exchange controls; that they should remove their controls on movements of capital; that real progress be made on freeing the internal market; and that inflation in the UK should be on a downward trend.)

Perhaps this, and other changes of tone, indicated that the balance of domestic political considerations had shifted. As well as the need to avert further dissension within the Cabinet, there was greater support for a more co-operative attitude within the Conservative Party, particularly in the aftermath of the elections to the European Parliament in June 1989, which the Conservatives had fought on a negative anti-Brussels platform, but which had proved something of a disaster for the Party (Table 3.1). Perhaps more importantly, there were indications of a change of mood amongst the electorate from which Labour, by posing as the more European of the two major parties, might well have been able to gain an advantage.

Table 3.1 Euro-election results, 15 June 1989

	Seats (UK) 1989 (1985)	Votes % (GB) 1989 (1985)	Votes % (GB) 1987
Conservative	32 (45)	34.7 (40.8)	43.3
Labour	45 (32)	40.1 (36.5)	31.5
Centre	– (–)	6.7 (19.5)	23.1
Green	– (–)	14.9 (0.6)	0.3
Other	4 (4)	3.6 (2.7)	1.8

Source: David Butler, 'Elections in Britain,' in Peter Caterall (ed.) *Contemporary Britain: An Annual Review 1990* (ICBH / Blackwell, London, 1990) p. 47.

The Labour Party

The transformation of Labour by the end of the 1980s into the more 'European' of the two major parties was quite remarkable, because throughout most of the post-war period it was Labour which had been the more divided party, with a consistent majority of the membership appearing to be hostile to European integration.

At the risk of some slight oversimplification, it can be said that the Labour Party was also divided into three factions on the issue of European integration. First there were the modernizers, who did not differ much in their beliefs from their counterparts within the Conservative Party. Secondly, there were the traditionalists, some of whom were more to the right of the Party, some more to the left, but who were united by a dislike of the idea of Britain becoming involved with Europe at all; they were progressive nationalists who believed in the multiracial Commonwealth as the only suitable international organization for Britain to co-operate with economically. Thirdly there were those on the left of the Party, who essentially saw the EC as a capitalist organization.

Macmillan's application divided the Labour Party, but the then leader, Hugh Gaitskell, came down firmly on the side of the opponents of membership. This probably reflected Gaitskell's own instincts: most politicians of that generation were imbued with the same sense of nationalism, and Gaitskell was also a firm believer in the ideal of a multi-racial Commonwealth. But it was also a politically opportune decision.

When the Government announced its decision to apply for membership, Gaitskell was engaged in an attempt to modernize the Labour Party, to get it to follow a similar route to that of the German Social Democratic Party. At its Bad Godesburg Congress in 1959 that Party had finally, after a long period of internal debate, abandoned its (purely theoretical) commitment to Marxism, and had accepted the legitimacy of the social market economy upon which the conservative (Christian Democrat) Government of the new Federal Republic of Germany had built the prosperity of the people and its own consequent electoral success.

The Labour Party had never drawn its inspiration from Marx, but it incorporated within its constitution a commitment to economic centralization and a hostility to the workings of the free market that was most graphically expressed in the Clause 4 commitment that a Labour Government would take state control of the 'commanding heights' of the economy. Gaitskell had wanted to get rid of that commitment, but his attack on Clause 4 had produced a serious split within the Party between the social democrats and the traditionalists. Nominally the victory went to the traditionalists: Clause 4 remained. In practice the battle paved the way for the modernization of the Party from which, after Gaitskell's untimely death, Harold Wilson was to benefit in the 1964 election.

When the issue of EC membership arose, the Party was still deeply divided over Clause 4, and also over the question of nuclear defence, which the leadership supported against strong opposition from the rank-and-file and the left of the Party. By coming out in opposition to British membership of the EC, a position favoured by the traditionalists, Gaitskell managed to avoid a further damaging split within the Party, and was able to strengthen his own position as leader after the battle over Clause 4. Following his speech to the 1962 Party Conference, in which he referred to the Conservative Government's application as a betrayal of a thousand years of history, 'the party united, found electoral confidence and ideological strength in its identity as the "Commonwealth" Party, and agreed to Gaitskell's continued leadership' (Robins, 1979, p. 41). This was the first instance of the internal politics of the Labour Party interacting with and possibly influencing the position of the leadership of the Party on British membership of the EC. It was not to be the last.

Wilson took over the legacy of Gaitskell when he became the leader of the Party. He had not been leader long when he became Prime Minister, which strengthened his position considerably. All the same, he faced determined opposition from within the Party when he decided to renew the British application for membership in 1966. Again, for party-political reasons there was no question of the application being defended in anything other than purely pragmatic terms, and the speed with which de Gaulle renewed his veto helped to dampen the ferocity of internal Party opposition. But it was clear from the reaction that a majority of Labour's membership, and probably of the Parliamentary Party too, opposed membership. This was an unexploded time bomb which Wilson took into opposition with him.

Having himself applied for membership while Prime Minister, it was difficult for Wilson flatly to oppose the application by the Heath Government, but it was also clear that if the Labour leader attempted to make the issue one of cross-party consensus he would not be able to hold his Party behind him. In these circumstances he came up with the ingenious compromise of opposing entry on the terms negotiated by the Conservative Government, and began to rehearse this theme as a running critique of the negotiations even before the final terms were agreed.

During Wilson's second spell as Prime Minister, in 1974–5, domestic politics came to be dominated by the issue of British membership of the EC, and Britain's attitude to the EC in turn came to be dominated by considerations of domestic politics.

The Labour Party in opposition had made a commitment that if returned to office it would renegotiate the terms of British entry to the EC and would put the new terms to the British people for their verdict. Eventually it was decided that the form of consultation would be a referendum.

This commitment guaranteed that the EC would figure prominently among the issues to be tackled by the new Government. Concentration on the EC suited Wilson: he inherited a country that was deeply divided along class lines, following the conflicts in the last years of Heath's premiership between the Government and the trade unions. The issue of membership of the EC was a welcome diversion from such matters, and because it divided the country along lines other than class, it offered a possible escape from the danger of such conflict becoming entrenched.

The issue also suited the left of the Labour Party, which following the disappointments of the first Wilson Governments had been strengthened, and had a new leading figure, the Cabinet Minister Tony Benn. The 'Bennite' left seemed intent on dislodging from leadership positions the pragmatic modernizers, the heirs of Gaitskell, who were now generally described as 'social democrats'. Their prime target was Roy Jenkins, the Deputy Leader. Membership of the EC was a good issue for the left to use in their attack on the social democrats. Unlike Gaitskell himself, the social democrats were united in support of EC membership; but they were in a minority in the Labour Party as a whole. On this issue it was possible for the left to win allies amongst Party members who were unsympathetic to other parts of their programme. The campaign would be sure to isolate the social democrats, and a decision to withdraw from the EC would be likely to precipitate their resignations (Bilski, 1977).

This whole strategy was predicated on the assumption that the British people would reject membership if given the choice in a referendum, an assumption that appeared reasonable from the evidence of opinion polls. But the left seriously underestimated the ability of an incumbent Prime Minister to sell even an unpopular policy to a majority of the electorate, if he had the backing of the leaders of the opposition parties and of a majority of the Press. The referendum produced a convincing two-thirds majority for continued membership on a two-thirds turn-out; as Wilson said, a more convincing majority than any British government had received in an election in the twentieth century (Wilson, 1979, p. 108).

Wilson's victory was bought at a price in terms of goodwill in the EC. The renegotiation produced few changes which could not have been achieved by normal diplomatic bargaining without the threat of withdrawal, but was conducted in the confrontational manner necessary to convince the British people that the Government was fighting vigorously on their behalf. Wilson, and his Foreign Secretary Callaghan, who did most of the negotiating, posed as national champions fighting the foreign enemy for a fairer deal. So successful was this approach in domestic political terms that it was to be imitated after 1979.

The referendum result did not put an end to opposition to the EC within the Labour Party, and Callaghan faced much the same constraints when he became Prime Minister. Consequently he adopted a tone in domestic discussion of the EC which was far from sympathetic to the idea of European integration, and which at times caused a certain amount of friction with his EC partners.

A good example was the letter that Callaghan sent to Ron Hayward, the Secretary of the Labour Party, before the 1977 Party Conference. In it the Prime Minister defended his Government's record in the EC in terms of its effectiveness in promoting the national interest; he acknowledged that there were continuing problems, but rejected withdrawal as a solution on the grounds that it would 'cause a profound upheaval in our relations with Europe, but also more widely in our relations with the United States'. This reasoning was hardly likely to endear him to Britain's European partners. Callaghan also defended the priority that Britain gave, during its first presidency of the Council of Ministers in 1977, to further enlargement of the EC on the grounds that 'The dangers of an over-centralized, over-bureaucratized and over-harmonized

Community will be far less with twelve than with nine' (*The Times*, 1 October 1977).

It has also been suggested that Callaghan's decision not to take sterling fully into the EMS when it was set up in 1978 was finally determined by the debate at the Labour Party Conference of that year, when speaker after speaker condemned the idea (Ludlow, 1982, pp. 217–18). However, it has already been argued in chapter 2 above that there were other reasons for that decision.

An issue on which domestic political considerations certainly did determine the Government's behaviour, though, was direct elections to the European Parliament. There was a clear commitment in the Treaty of Rome to move from the indirectly elected Assembly, which consisted of national members of parliament who were seconded to sit in Luxembourg, to a directly elected institution. At a meeting of the European Council in September 1976, this was firmed up into an agreement to hold direct elections in 1978. Callaghan's acceptance of this commitment may have been in fulfilment of some sort of deal made by Wilson with French President Giscard d'Estaing to secure France's agreement to the renegotiated terms of entry.

Whatever the reason, Callaghan did not take the steps necessary to introduce into the Westminster Parliament the legislation that would make it possible to hold the elections in Britain. The thinking behind this almost certainly concerned domestic politics. The hostility exhibited towards the idea of direct elections at the 1976 Labour Party Conference may have had some influence. But the main factor was that Callaghan was working with a slender majority in Parliament and needed to ensure the support of his backbench MPs for a domestic economic programme that was not tremendously popular with them; he therefore did not want to antagonize them unduly. Also, even amongst pro-EC members of the Cabinet there was some doubt about holding such elections in 1978. All the indications were that Labour might do badly in elections held then (Whitehead, 1977, pp. 275–6).

Moves were only made to implement the Brussels commitment when the Government's majority finally disappeared, and Callaghan was obliged to turn to the Liberals for support. David Steel, the Liberal leader, made it a condition of sustaining the Government in office that enabling legislation be introduced as soon as possible and that the elections be held under a system of proportional representation (Steel, 1980, p. 39). Callaghan was unable to deliver on the second of these conditions, but he went as far as he could in allowing a free vote on the issue and supporting proportional representation himself, contrary to a lifelong personal preference for the traditional British first-past-the-post system.

Because the Conservatives supported the introduction of direct elections, the legislation went through against opposition from the Labour backbenches; but the proportional representation system was not adopted, which meant that the Boundary Commission had to draw up European constituencies, with a consequent delay which meant that the first direct elections had to be postponed until 1979 throughout the EC.

With the exception of this issue, though, the policies of the Callaghan Government towards the EC were less obviously driven by domestic political considerations than had been those of the Wilson Governments. What was certainly affected by domestic considerations, though, was the tone of the Government's statements on the issue, which remained predominantly negative and narrowly nationalistic. The same phenomenon was to appear again with the Conservative Government that succeeded to office in 1979.

Following the 1979 election defeat the left regained the initiative in the internal struggle within the Party, and pushed through a number of reforms which alienated and marginalized the social democrats. But the issue which split the Party, and led several prominent social democrats to leave to form the Social Democratic Party (SDP), was again the EC.

In 1980 the left achieved a major success in getting Michael Foot elected as leader of the Labour Party. Although Foot was generally thought of as being on the left, he was never part of what came to be known as the 'hard left'; but he was indulgent towards parts of the programme of the hard left; and he was a long-standing opponent of British membership of the EC. His opposition to the EC was much more that of a traditionalist than of a left-wing socialist: his main argument against membership was that it would undermine the sovereignty of Parliament and the established system of parliamentary democracy, rather than its implications for the viability of a socialist economic programme (Foot, 1975). But with the sympathy of the leader, and the defection of leading pro-European figures to the SDP, the left was able to get withdrawal from the EC accepted as Party policy, and it was part of the manifesto on which Labour fought the 1983 election.

That election was disastrous for Labour, and was quickly followed by Foot's resignation. Neil Kinnock, who succeeded Foot, was thought to be from a similar point on the political spectrum, but he soon showed that he was intent on pragmatically reforming Labour to turn it back into a credible party of government. The process of policy review under Kinnock included a change of attitude to the EC. Opposition to continued membership in 1983 had been successfully presented by the Conservatives as evidence of Labour's lack of realism; to make the Party's claim to be an alternative party of Government credible, some policy had to be developed which would involve a positive view of Britain's future in the EC, to replace the negativism of the policy of withdrawal. But the change in the attitude of the Party to the point where it could end the 1980s being seen as the more 'European' of the two major parties was due to three circumstances.

First, the strongly nationalistic tone adopted by Thatcher in her approach to the European integration made it difficult for Labour to criticise the Conservatives for selling out the national interest; yet as divisions emerged within the Conservative Party over the EC, it was increasingly difficult for the Labour leadership to turn down the opportunity to embarrass the Government, which was much easier to do from a pro-EC than an anti-EC direction.

Secondly, just as the intense hostility generated by Heath's attempts at reforming industrial relations had spilled over into a rejection by Labour's supporters of Heath's policy of EC membership, so Thatcher's attacks on the trade unions and other natural Labour supporters led to a resentment that extended to antagonism to her apparent discord with the EC.

Thirdly, there was a shift in thinking on the left of the Party. Whereas the left in the late 1970s and early 1980s championed an 'Alternative Economic Strategy' that involved import controls and other economic protectionist measures which were incompatible with membership of the EC, the failure of the reflationary strategy of the French Socialist Government in the early 1980s sparked off an intellectual reassessment of the possibility of one government being able to act alone to control the effects of what was an increasingly interdependent European economy. There was increasing recognition that the existence of multinational corporations, and the internationalization of banks and financial markets, meant that the nation-state was no longer able to regulate these structures (Rosamond, 1990).

Perhaps the most important factor in the reorientation of Labour, though, was the gradual conversion of the trade unions to a more sympathetic attitude to the EC. This was based on experience of working with other European unions in the European Trade Union Confederation, and on direct experience of participation within the various committees and working parties of the EC itself. This experience was combined with a growing awareness that there was an opportunity to realize some of the social objectives of trade unionism through the EC, where there was no prospect of doing so through influencing the British Conservative Government.

This factor was highlighted by the dispute over the social charter. The proposals in the Commission's charter covered most of the objectives of the British trade unions in terms of fair wages, decent working conditions, and participation in industrial decision-making. Thatcher's rejection of the proposals was contrasted with the personal championing of them at the 1988 Trades Union Congress by the President of the Commission, Jacques Delors, after which he received a standing ovation; and with the acceptance of the charter by the governments of almost all the other member states.

Although the policy review document left room to doubt

whether Labour's conversion to Europeanism was as complete as the popular perception of it (Rosamond, 1990), there was no doubt that by the end of the 1980s Labour had changed considerably in its stance towards the EC from the situation in 1974 when Michael Foot, then Secretary of State for Employment, 'vetoed an employment protection regulation otherwise quite in accord with Labour thinking, rather than accept such reforms at the hands of the Community.' (Grahl and Teague, 1988, p. 73).

Conclusion

British politicians of both major parties fought shy of embracing the ideal of European integration. Partly this may have been for electoral reasons: public opinion in Britain only slowly came round to acceptance of the EC. But there is something of a 'chicken-and-egg' dilemma here. Was the electorate unenthusiastic about European integration because its political leaders did not give it a lead in that direction? The result of the 1975 referendum on membership would seem to indicate that when the political leaders gave a positive indication that the electorate should support EC membership, that lead was followed (Pierce, Valen, and Listhaug, 1983). More often, though, political leaders adopted anti-EC stances for short-term gain. This certainly applied to Harold Wilson, both before and after the referendum, and to Margaret Thatcher.

Both Conservative and Labour leaders, though, would have faced tremendous problems within their own parties had they embraced European integration too warmly. Within the Conservative Party the strength of the ideal of nationalism, not just on the right of the Party but with the bulk of the ordinary members, was such that neither Macmillan nor Heath could risk ever appearing to sacrifice the national interest for the ideal of European integration. Within the Labour Party the strength of opposition to membership was based on both nationalism and a view of the EC as a capitalist organization that was inimical to the interests of workers.

After 1979 positions began slowly to change. The strength of Thatcher's apparent hostility to the EC was initially functional in strengthening her own position as a right wing leader; but as it came to threaten Britain with isolation within the EC, and to alarm sections of both financial and industrial capital with the prospect of partial exclusion from the full benefits of the post-1992 single market, so opposition to her stance began to build up within the Party.

At the same time, Thatcher's opposition to developments in the EC encouraged Labour to look on it more sympathetically, especially because some of the objectives of the social dimension of 1992, which Thatcher hotly resisted, coincided with the objectives which the labour movement hoped to achieve in Britain.

4 The Effects of EC Membership

Although successive British governments endeavoured to minimize the impact on the country of membership of the EC, it has meant taking part in the process of European integration, which has had an effect on the constitution, the degree of democratic control of the executive, the structure and functioning of the national economy, and increasingly on other areas of policy.

Constitutional effects

When Britain entered the EC it became part of a new constitutional order that was based on very different principles from those that governed the United Kingdom of Great Britain and Northern Ireland. It is likely that few people realized the full extent of the constitutional issues that membership raised, although amongst the opponents of membership there were those who sounded warnings, notably Enoch Powell and Michael Foot (Powell, 1975; Foot, 1975). The problem of reconciling British and EC constitutional principles has still not been resolved entirely satisfactorily.

Britain prior to membership had no formal written constitution: but the EC had the founding Treaties, to which has been added since 1987 the Single European Act. These documents act as a written constitution against which the actions of

the decision-making institutions and of the member states can
be judged. The body that sits in judgement is the European
Court of Justice.

As every textbook on the subject warns, this Court, which
sits in Luxembourg, should not be confused with the European
Court of Human Rights, which is an institution of the Council
of Europe and sits in Strasbourg. The Court of Justice consists
of thirteen judges, one from each member state plus one extra,
because an even number of judges would raise the possibility
of there being split decisions. Each judge is appointed for a
six-year term of office, with the appointments being staggered
to ensure continuity. The judges are assisted by six advocates
general, one of whom presents before the Court the legal
arguments raised by each case (Nugent, 1989, pp. 160–1).

In the constitutional arrangements of the EC, the Court
plays a role directly equivalent to that of the Supreme Court in
the United States of America, and just as the US Supreme
Court in the last century consistently promoted federalism, the
European Court has used its power to interpret a written
constitution in ways that have consistently promoted European
integration (Schermers, 1974).

From the point of view of compatibility with British constitutional principles, the most important doctrine that the Court
has established is that Community law must always take precedence over national law where there is any conflict. This was
already a well-established and clear principle before British
entry. It had been laid down in the case of *Costa v ENEL* in
1964, and repeatedly reasserted. (Freestone, 1983, p. 48). The
logic of the argument is that the nature of EC law requires that
it should be the same in all parts of the Community, otherwise
it would cease to be genuine Community law. This seems
clear, since if every legislative act of the Council of Ministers
could be overruled where it conflicted with a particular national
law, there could be as many different versions of EC law as
there were member states. However, the doctrine that EC law
overrides national law wherever there is a conflict directly
contradicts the British constitutional principle of the sovereignty
of Parliament.

It is a fundamental tenet of the uncodified British constitution that Parliament is sovereign. This means that there is no source of law which is more fundamental than an Act of Parliament. There are other sources of law, such as the common law for example, of which everybody has heard through the phrase 'common-law wife'. But the common law, and any other sort of law, only applies so long as it does not come into conflict with statutes of Parliament. As soon as a conflict arises between a statute and some other form of law, the judiciary is obliged, according to the doctrine of parliamentary sovereignty, to give precedence to the statute.

A second aspect of the doctrine is the principle *lex posterior derogat priori*, or in English 'the later law overrides the earlier'. This principle is also presented as 'no parliament can bind its successor', because its implication is that if two statutes come into conflict, the Courts are obliged to give precedence to the one passed later in time. To give an example, if a future Labour Government were to renationalize one or more of the once publicly-owned utilities that the Thatcher Conservative Governments had privatized, no shareholder could claim against the Government in law on the grounds of rights acquired under the privatization Act, because the renationalization Act, being the later to be passed, would take precedence. This principle is clearly necessary if the democratic principle is to prevail, that at an election the people can turn out of office an unpopular Government and install a majority in Parliament supporting in office a Government of a different political complexion.

Britain differs from most continental European countries in making Parliament supreme in this manner. Most other states have a category of law which is more fundamental than statute law, in the form of a written constitution, sometimes with entrenched provisions on human rights. Membership of the EC has posed particular problems for the doctrine of the sovereignty of Parliament, because it has introduced a category of law which, according to the interpretation of the European Court of Justice, is more fundamental than statute, namely EC law.

There is a constitutional quandary here for the Courts.

According to British constitutional tradition, European Community law only has the force of law in the United Kingdom by virtue of the European Communities Act 1972, since international treaties do not become domestic law until embodied by statute. So, on the principle of *lex posterior derogat priori*, the Courts ought to react to any conflict between Community law and national law by treating any national law that was passed later than 1972 as the one that prevails. Under the different constitutional order of the EC, however, as interpreted by the Court of Justice, the Community law should prevail (Mitchell, 1979; George, 1980).

After a period of inconsistency in judgments from different Courts, the judiciary appear to have got around this difficulty by treating the Court of Justice's doctrine as a 'rule of construction'. This means the Courts will assume that Parliament could not have meant to contradict a Community law unless there is an explicit statement to that effect in the preamble of the statute concerned. They can therefore give precedence to Community law in a case of conflict without having to overturn centuries of British constitutional tradition (Steiner, 1990, chs. 2 & 3).

Despite this ingenious device for reconciling two apparently contradictory principles, the fact remains that citizens of the United Kingdom now live under laws that are made in Brussels as well as laws that are made at Westminster. Whether this constitutes a weakening of our democratic system depends on how far Parliament is able to exercise control over the EC-level process of making decisions.

Parliamentary scrutiny of EC legislation

The two Houses of Parliament have adopted different approaches to the scrutiny of European legislation. The Select Committee on the European Communities of the House of Lords considers matters of Community business which it judges to be important, and prepares reports for the full House. The Select Committee on European Legislation (previously the Select Committee on European Secondary Legislation) of the House of Commons does not itself prepare detailed opinions on EC draft legislation. It sifts the proposals coming before the Council of Ministers, and divides them into those which are relatively minor in its opinion, and those which are deserving of consideration by the whole House (Kolinsky, 1975; Brew, 1979). Control of the executive lies predominantly in the House of Commons, and it is to the work of that House's Select Committee (often called the 'Scrutiny Committee') that the comments below are addressed.

When the procedure first began to operate there were serious teething troubles, and it did look as though effective control over the executive had been lost in this area. Debates on matters of EC business which the Select Committee chose for further consideration were held late at night, and were sparsely attended. They were given little time, and because of the tremendous backlog of business already outstanding when the Committee got to work, the debates took place very late in the decision-making process of the Community. This resulted in some decisions being made in the Council of Ministers before the House had debated the issues.

On 30 October 1980 a Resolution of the House expressed the opinion that no Minister of the Crown should give agreement in the Council of Ministers to any proposal which had been recommended by the Committee for debate by the House before the debate had been held, unless the Committee had agreed to this or the Minister concerned decided that there were special reasons for not withholding agreement; and in the latter case the Minister should take the first available opportunity to explain the reasons to the House. In August 1984, in replying to the 1983–4 Special Report of the Committee, the Government made a statement of policy that it would consider the Resolution of October 1980 to apply to proposals not yet scrutinized by the Committee. Generally these principles were adhered to, although in its Second Special Report for 1985–6 the Committee had cause to complain about two instances of the agreed procedure being flouted, both involving the Department of Trade and Industry.

The Single European Act increased the workload of the Committee, because it gave the European Parliament an increased power to amend proposals relating to the freeing of the internal market by the end of 1992, which in the Council of Ministers came under the Act's majority-voting rules. Where proposals that had been considered by the Committee were subsequently amended by the European Parliament, the amended proposals had to be looked at again by the Committee.

In its Second Special Report for 1985−6, the Committee expressed its concern that the House was not being adequately informed on Community affairs. It quoted the Single European Act as an example. The House had had no opportunity to comment on the provisions of the Act prior to its being agreed by Heads of Government. The Committee's terms of reference had debarred it from reporting on the Act or on the Inter-Governmental Conference which produced it. Similarly, Inter-Governmental Agreements to increase the resources of the Community fell outside the Committee's terms of reference. The increasing complexity of the workings of the Community, the accelerated pace of developments in pursuit of the 1992 deadline for freeing the internal market, the tendency of issues arising within the Community to fall outside the terms of reference of any single Departmental Select Committee, and the necessarily intermittent attention which those committees could give to Community affairs, all indicated to the Scrutiny Committee the need for its own terms of reference to be broadened to allow it to report to the House on developments within the Community of which the House should be aware, to provide assessments of the likely significance of these developments for the United Kingdom, and to issue more detailed reports on selected documents or matters, in the manner of the House of Lords' Committee.

The Government in its reply to this Report was not prepared to concede the proposed extension of the terms of reference, saying that in its opinion the time was not ripe for such an extension. However, in response to pressure from the Chairmen of other Commons' Committees, and to considerable concern expressed by backbenchers on both sides of the House, the

Leader of the House agreed in July 1989 that he was willing to provide the Committee with a wider range of documents than just those specified in its terms of reference, and would take steps to remove procedural impediments to such documents being further considered by the House as though they were European Community Documents as defined in the Committee's standing orders, thereby conceding a *de facto* extension of the Committee's competence. The Chairman indicated the Committee's willingness to proceed on this basis without prejudice to its general position, on the understanding that the Government would review the position after a reasonable time if the Committee did not find it satisfactory.

Two other Commons committees regularly monitored developments in the EC from the start of British membership: the Select Committee on Foreign Affairs and the Treasury Select Committee. They took evidence on EC matters relevant to the work of the Foreign Office and the Treasury respectively, and issued reports on developments in government policy towards the EC. But this was only one aspect of their work, and although they were able to investigate issues that fell outside the remit of the Scrutiny Committee, it was less than satisfactory in the view of some parliamentarians that no single committee had a brief to oversee EC developments.

Despite considerable evidence that scrutiny was not working well, the Select Committee on Procedure, in its Fourth Report for Session 1988–9, dated 8 November 1989, did not support the further extension of the remit of the Scrutiny Committee, nor the creation of either a new Select Committee on European Affairs or a Standing Committee to oversee all EC documents. Instead it strongly urged Departmental Select Committees to consider setting up sub-committees on European legislation, and proposed the creation of five special Standing Committees on European documents relating to agriculture, trade and industry, Treasury matters, transport and the environment, and general legislation, as a means of allowing some of the debate on EC matters to take place outside of the Chamber, where time was limited. The Government accepted these recommendations in essence, only questioning the number of new

Standing Committees, on the grounds that it might be difficult to find enough members with the interest and expertise to operate five such committees, and suggesting that intially three might be a more feasible target. Subsequently three new Standing Committees were created.

Overall, parliamentary oversight of the executive had just about been maintained in matters relating to Community business prior to the passing of the Single European Act, although at the cost of a considerable commitment of time by parliamentarians and parliamentary clerical staff. As F.E.C. Gregory put it: 'What E.C membership has done is to add a range of new problems to a legislature that already felt itself to be staggering under the pressure of domestic legislation and executive domination' (Gregory, 1973, p. 122).

Nevertheless, by the end of the 1980s there was a widespread feeling in elite circles that a 'democratic deficit' had opened up with respect to EC legislation, especially following the agreement in the Single European Act to adopt weighted majority voting in the Council of Ministers over a range of matters relating to the freeing of the internal market. Once a national government could be outvoted, it was difficult to sustain the argument that democratic control had been maintained. Parliament might express a clear and unequivocal view against adoption of a specific proposal from the Commission, but the Government would not be able to ensure that that view prevailed when the matter was voted on in the Council of Ministers. One conclusion that could be drawn was that the existence of such a democratic deficit strengthened the case for extending the legislative powers of the European Parliament, as the only directly elected body which could realistically act as a check on the joint Commission/Council executive of the EC as a whole.

Many British parliamentarians, however, remained reluctant to see the powers of the European Parliament increased, believing that this would be the first step to reducing the status of the Westminster Parliament. What this argument ignored was the reality that developments in the EC had already passed the point where complete democratic control could be exercised from Westminster, so that the proponents of increasing the powers of the European Parliament appeared to be correct in saying that the choice was between effective democratic control at the European level, or no effective democratic control at all.

Economic effects

It was always obvious that membership of the EC would have economic consequences for Britain. What these might be was central to the debate that took place at the time of entry and during the referendum campaign. An attempt is made here to estimate what those effects had been by the end of the 1980s, although this is no easy task because other factors had influenced the development of the British economy in addition to membership of the EC.

Trade

Perhaps the most obvious economic effect of membership was a change in both the intensity and pattern of British trade, although even here other influences were at work.

By 1986, following the accession to membership of Spain and Portugal, around half of Britain's total trade, both imports and exports, was with the rest of the EC. In comparison, in the mid-1960s the states that today form the EC accounted for less than 20 per cent of Britain's total trade. At that time British trade still reflected the legacy of Empire and Commonwealth links, with manufactured goods representing only 44 per cent of imports but 84 per cent of exports. This was a pattern of trade that involved importing food, fuel, and raw materials and converting them into finished exports of manufactures. By the mid-1980s the picture had changed significantly: manufactures still accounted for nearly 75 per cent of exports, but they also accounted for some 73 per cent of imports (Smith, 1987).

Changes in both the geographical pattern of trade and its composition reflected membership of the EC. The removal of tariffs increased the likelihood that Britain would both export more to and import more from the EC. Some of this changed geographical pattern represented a diversion of trade from other parts of the world, but some of it also was the result of trade creation consequent on being part of a highly interdependent economic zone. In particular, the increasing domination of industrial production by large multinational corporations led to a pattern of trade which partly reflected the tendency of such companies to split their production process between plants in different countries and then trade with themselves in bringing the components together into a finished product. This was a trend that was particularly obvious in the motor vehicle industry, with several manufacturers operating integrated production on a cross-national basis. That Britain shared in this new division of labour was at least partly due to its being part of the EC, where disruption to such 'internal' trade by the erection of tariff barriers was impossible.

Despite this degree of integration in trade with the rest of the EC, in the 1980s Britain was not the leading trading partner of any other member state except Ireland, and still did more of its trade outside of the EC than any other member state except the new entrants (Wallace, 1984, p. 18). On the other hand, by the end of the decade the Federal Republic of Germany had overtaken the United States as Britain's leading trading partner.

What was worrying was that this German predominance in trade with Britain was based on a tremendous surge in German exports to Britain, resulting in a considerable British trade deficit. Partly this seemed to be the result of the decline in Britain's indigenous capital goods industries, which meant that when British industry wished to renew and increase its stock of plant and machinery it had to import to do so. Those imports, which previously might have come from the United States, by the 1980s were much more likely to come from Germany. But partly also the deficits resulted from a decline in the value of exports of North Sea oil, as the price of oil fell in real terms.

Dependence on exports of oil, a finite resource, had been a worrying trend in Britain's trade with the rest of the EC for

some time. But it is doubtful whether the weakness of manufacturing industry could be blamed simply on British membership of the EC. Since 1979 the policies of the Conservative
Governments had emphasized the need to keep the British
economy open to the world, and not to use government subsidies
or other forms of assistance artificially to sustain any particular
economic sector. The record of British industry in exporting to
the rest of the EC may not have been good, and the level of
imports of manufactured goods from the EC had risen steadily:
but the record of trade in manufactures with the rest of the
world had not been good either, despite a certain amount of
protection offered by the common external tariff of the EC.
Without EC membership it is unlikely that manufacturing
industry would have fared any better given the open trading
policies adopted by the Government of the period.

Where Britain may have suffered economically is in the
failure of the EC to achieve the same sort of free trade in
services that it had in manufactured goods, particularly in
financial services and air transport where Britain appeared to
have a comparative advantage. This explains the Government's
enthusiasm for those aspects of the 1992 programme that
referred to the freedom of services, and there was the prospect
that with the completion of this programme the British balance
of payments position relative to the EC might improve, even if
the balance of trade remained in deficit.

Direct investment

Turning from trade to direct investment, although Britain by
the end of the 1980s conducted half of all its trade with the
EC, the pattern of inward and outward investment flows was
much more widely dispersed. British companies were the
largest foreign investors in the United States, exceeding the
Japanese. At the same time Japanese companies had become
substantial investors in Britain.

This Japanese inward investment was attracted to Britain by
a variety of factors, but the reasons why the Japanese came to

Britain were clearly headed by the fact that Britain was a member of the EC. Had it not been a member, then there is little doubt that the investment would have gone elsewhere, to a site inside the EC. The attractions of Britain, including particularly a government that was more sympathetic to such foreign investment than its counterparts in several other EC states, were reasons why the Japanese invested in that particular part of the EC; but it was most important for those companies to be inside the large EC market. The British market itself was only a starting point for penetration of the rest of the EC. For this reason, governments in other European countries sometimes felt that Britain was acting as a Trojan horse for Japan. But it could not act as a Trojan horse were it not within the walls.

Agriculture

Perhaps the biggest difficulty for Britain to result from late entry to the EC was the common agricultural policy. It was the cause of the imbalance in Britain's net payments to the Community's budget, and it figured prominently in the debate on entry because of the predicted effect on food prices. The system also encouraged a restructuring of British agriculture.

Food prices were a particularly sensitive political issue at the time of the membership applications and the referendum. All states followed some sort of protectionist and interventionist policy for agriculture. The traditional British system was one of deficiency payments, in which food prices were allowed to find their own level, and farmers were compensated for any shortfall in their incomes by direct payments from the government. The system managed to keep food prices low while ensuring stability of farmers' incomes, and it allowed the government to bring pressure to bear on individual farmers to improve their efficiency. The subsidy came from the taxpayer, and as the British system of taxation placed the emphasis on progressive income tax, this meant that the richer citizens paid more towards the subsidy than the poorer.

The system that had been adopted by the Community was based on guaranteed prices. Every year national Ministers of Agriculture decided on the level of prices for the products covered by the common agricultural policy. If prices fell below the agreed levels, the Commission would intervene in the market to buy up surplus produce, which was then placed into storage. If prices were above the level prevailing in world markets, subsidies were paid to farmers who exported their produce to bring their receipts up to the level that they would get if they were selling in the Community market.

This arrangement implied a large increase in the general price of food in the country, a problem that the Heath Government accepted as insuperable. The agricultural policy had to be accepted if membership were to be achieved. In any case, the British system was proving to be a cause of financial difficulty, and as early as 1960 Christopher Soames, then Minister of Agriculture, had advised Macmillan that some change, passing more of the cost on to the consumer, seemed essential irrespective of any move to join the EC (Charlton, 1983, p. 243). The negotiators therefore concentrated on achieving a satisfactory period for phasing in the full effects of the policy on prices, and on getting agreement to special concessions on certain particularly sensitive items like butter. The 1970 Government White Paper (Cmnd. 4289) estimated that the full application of the common agricultural policy in Britain would result in an increase of between 18 and 26 per cent in food prices; the 1971 White Paper (Cmnd. 4715) estimated 16 per cent.

At the time of the referendum the sting was taken out of the argument about the price of food because during 1975 the price of food on world markets rose remarkably. This was a consequence of rather specific circumstances, including a coincidence of bad harvests in various parts of the world. But it did allow the proponents of membership to argue that the era of cheap food was at an end (Williams, 1975). In fact, some products were actualy selling within the EC at guaranteed prices which were lower than world market prices.

Following these somewhat unusual conditions in the mid-

1970s, world prices returned to levels well below those guaranteed under the common agricultural policy, and it was calculated that by the late 1980s the British consumer was paying something like 20 per cent above world prices for food (Martin, 1988, p. 16). But the issue did not return to the level of political debate, partly because food was cheaper in relation to earnings than it had been in the 1970s. In 1987 the average British manual worker earned enough to buy a loaf of bread in 6.2 minutes, compared with 8.4 minutes in 1974; the cost of a pint of milk was earned in 3.6 minutes, compared with 4.2 minutes in 1974; and the same applied to other foodstuffs, including meat (*The Times*, 15 December 1987).

How far the higher cost of food was a direct consequence of membership of the EC is not entirely clear, given the evidence already quoted above, that as early as 1960 the old British system of deficiency payments had become too expensive to sustain for much longer. Presumably even without membership there would have been some increase in prices, as subsidies were reduced in line with increasing incomes. It is also not clear how much the increased incomes owed to EC membership; so the record on this issue does not allow us to judge whether the effect of membership was on balance positive or negative.

An effect of the common agricultural policy that was not discussed at the time of the referendum was that on the structure of British agriculture. The policy was thought of in Britain as a system that benefited small inefficient peasant farmers, but this was a somewhat misleading impression. The major beneficiaries of the system were always the large-scale efficient farmers. Because guaranteed prices were set for political reasons at a level that would sustain the small and inefficient farmer in business, they provided the large and efficient farmers, whose costs of production were much lower, with super-profits over and above what was needed to keep them in business.

The consequence of the application of this system to British agriculture was the purchase of agricultural holdings by large financial institutions. Farm sizes increased, and in the grain-growing areas of East Anglia the face of the countryside was transformed as hedgerows were torn out, at considerable cost to the environment, to allow uninterrupted ploughing and planting of large fields. British self-sufficiency in food increased from 60 per cent to 80 per cent overall, and for the first time in history mainland Britain became a net exporter of grain.

Effects on environmental policy

Because the protection of the environment has clear economic implications, it is an area with which the EC has always concerned itself. After 1972, when environmental awareness was raised considerably by the United Nations Stockholm Conference, there was an increasing emphasis on the environmental aspect of the EC.

For Britain the relevance of the EC to environmental questions was less obvious than it was for member states on the Continent, where pollution was more obviously an issue which escaped national control, as was shown by the pollution of the Rhine in 1986. Even here it was not obvious that the EC was the best forum through which to co-ordinate anti-pollution measures: the pollution of the Rhine was the result of a release into it of effluent from within Switzerland, a non-member of the EC. But the need for anti-pollution measures to be legally binding arose because all such measures cost industry money to implement, and so an equality of cleanliness was necessary to preserve the 'level playing field' of fair competition.

On several occasions the British Government found itself in conflict with the EC on environmental matters. In 1975 the Wilson Government, straight after the referendum, found itself in dispute with the Commission on the question of the pollution of rivers. The Commission had proposed to the Council of Ministers that there should be maximum legal limits on the emission of pollutants into rivers; the British maintained that these were inappropriate for Britain, which as an island had faster flowing rivers that cleared pollution more swiftly than could the rivers of the continental land-mass, and could therefore take more effluent. There was some validity in this argument: as islands, Britain and Ireland differ from their continental partners on a whole variety of environmental and health issues. On the other hand, the suspicion in Brussels and other national capitals was that the British Government had been influenced by the British chemical industry, which had balked at the cost of implementing the Commission's proposals. Yet it was precisely the cost which was the major issue for competitors of Britain's chemical industry, particularly West Germany. If British firms were allowed to get away with laxer emission standards, they would be given a cost-advantage over their continental competitors (George, 1990, p. 97).

On this occasion the British argument was eventually accepted, so membership of the EC did less than it might have to protect the British environment: but the incident generated a certain amount of ill-will amongst other member states towards such arguments from the British, and made it less likely that they would be able to gain exemption from generally agreed controls in the future.

Another incident that had an effect in Britain concerned airborne pollutants. Here Britain was seen as a major offender, because emissions of noxious gasses from its coal-fired power stations were identified as a major cause of acid rain in north-western Europe. This question became particularly important for the West Germans in the 1980s, with the rise of the Green movement and widespread concern amongst the German people about the death of their forests. Here pollution control became a matter of international diplomacy, and it is likely that Britain would have accepted the need to impose controls for reasons of maintaining good bilateral relations with the Germans even had the country not been a member of the EC. However, membership did increase the urgency of the issue, since it drove a wedge between Britain and Germany in the game of alliances and bargaining in other forums within the EC.

In 1989, with the environment high on the domestic policy agenda, EC regulations on the purity of drinking water became an issue of political concern. In October the Commission announced that it was taking Britain to the Court of Justice over its failure to achieve the required standards. The move was a blow to the Government's already tarnished image as a defender of the environment, but what made matters worse was that the water-supply industry was scheduled for privatization, a move that had already proved unpopular even with Conservative voters. The Commission's action made a succesful sale to the private sector less likely, and threatened to undermine the privatization advertising campaign.

On more than one occasion, then, the EC's attempts at environmental protection caused difficulties for British governments either in their relations with the rest of the EC or in domestic political terms. Overall it is probably true that EC membership resulted in a higher level of environmental protection than would otherwise have been voluntarily adopted, although it is difficult to be sure what the position would have been had Britain not been a member of the EC. And such positive steps as did result from the obligations of membership need to be set against the negative effects on the ecology and appearance of the English countryside in those areas that were most affected by the intensive farming methods that were encouraged by the common agricultural policy prior to its reform.

Effects on social policy

Perhaps the most obvious effect on social policy in Britain of membership of the EC was in the field of women's rights in the workplace. When Britain joined there was already a body of EC legislation on this subject, which went beyond what was available under national law. Successive British governments, however, resisted further measures of social legislation at EC level, except in so far as they involved the freedom of people to live and work in different parts of the Community.

A commitment to equal pay for men and women was written into the Treaty of Rome (EEC) mainly at the insistence of France, which was concerned that its existing generous provisions should not result in its industry having to bear higher costs than others in the EC. The matter was taken up and pushed by the Commission only in the course of the 1960s as women became a more important part of the labour force throughout Europe. A big step forward was taken in 1975 when a directive was accepted which established a wider definition of equal pay, and compelled member states to repeal legislation incompatible with EC policy, to refuse to accept collective agreements which did not incorporate equal pay, and to provide proper information to working women on their rights, together with a formal claims procedure (Collins, 1983, p. 106).

These measures in the realm of equal pay were supplemented by a 1976 directive requiring equal access for men and women to employment, training, and promotion; and by a 1979 directive requiring the progressive implementation of equality for men and women in social security schemes. These measures were agreed by British Labour Governments, and though they would almost certainly not have been accepted by the Thatcher Conservative Governments, they were implemented in Britain. This led women's groups to adopt a more positive attitude towards the EC, seeing that the cause of women's equality had been helped by membership.

The negative attitude of the Thatcher Governments to EC social legislation was graphically illustrated by an attempt that was made during the 1986 British presidency of the Council of Ministers to shift the whole emphasis of employment policy away from the protection of workers' rights and towards the freeing of the market in labour.

The ideas of the British Government were contained in a 19-page document entitled *Employment Growth into the 1990s: A Strategy for the Labour Market*. The plan proposed concentrating the work of the Council of Employment Ministers on job creation, to combat the high level of unemployment in the EC. It presented a four-point plan which involved aid for small businesses and the self-employed, the encouragement of more flexible working practices, better training, and more help for the long-term unemployed to find jobs. The approach was distinctly Thatcherite in its emphasis on freeing the market, and was too indifferent to the rights of workers to be acceptable to a majority of the other member states (George, 1990, pp. 187–8).

During 1989 the gulf between Britain and the rest of the EC on the social dimension of 1992 became one of the two major issues (the other being progress to monetary union) around which dispute centred. The Commission's 'social charter' of workers' rights, seen by most of the other member states as essential to the success of the whole process of freeing the internal maket, was adopted at the Strasbourg meeting of the European Council by eleven votes to Britain's one. This resistance to allowing the EC to affect the social policy of the United Kingdom was also expressed in British insistence that the Lingua programme for language training should not be extended from the tertiary level to the primary and secondary levels of education, where the Commission was given no competence under the Treaty of Rome.

This latter issue indicated that there was more at stake in the 'social charter' dispute than just the difference between Britain and the rest of the EC over what the appropriate level of social provision ought to be: there was also a constitutional issue concerning the competence of the EC to legislate at all in certain areas. At the time of writing, this constitutional dispute was unresolved, but upon its resolution rested the question of to what extent Britain's social policy in the future would be further affected by membership of the EC. If even a part of the social legislation mooted in the social charter were implemented, the effects on Britain could be far-reaching in comparison with the sort of provision that the Conservative Government would willingly make.

Conclusion

In the debate about the effects of entry that took place in 1975, at the time of the British referendum, predictions were made on both sides of the argument, the validity of which remained difficult to assess even fifteen years later (George, 1989). What had become clear, though, was that the constitutional effects were as fundamental as some of the opponents of membership had argued; and that an increasing number of domestic policy areas had assumed a significant European dimension. The effects of membership on the economy, though, were difficult to separate from the effects of other factors.

Membership of the EC brought more far-reaching consequences for Britain than were anticipated when the applications were made, consequences which at the end of the 1980s looked likely to be further extended after 1992. These consequences were the result of Britain participating in a process of European integration which went further than the somewhat limited objectives of British governments. Despite the efforts of successive governments to limit the effects of membership, there was little room to doubt that British sovereignty had been diminished by membership of the EC, and that it would be diminished further.

5 Conclusion

'European integration' is a term open to differing interpretations. Within the British governing elite there long prevailed an image of the form that European integration should take. It should be confined largely to economic integration, to be achieved through the creation of a free-trade area in Europe that would be a precursor of a world free-trade area. Politically the only form of integration that has been favoured by British governments of different political hues has been co-operation between sovereign states to achieve more effectively their common goals in foreign policy.

In pursuit of this limited definition of integration, British governments in the 1950s supported the development of the intergovernmental OEEC as the main vehicle of European unity, and withdrew support from the more far-reaching schemes for the development of the Council of Europe as a European federal governing body.

This minimalist view contrasted with the view that became dominant amongst the six original member states of the EC. They adopted a more interventionist approach to economic integration, modifying free trade through centrally agreed and implemented common policies. This approach was later embraced by Ireland, Greece, Spain, and Portugal, all of whom stood to benefit from redistributive policies. Movement beyond free trade was also envisaged in the plans for an economic and monetary union.

Politically, the idea of economic integration as only a step on the road to a European union had a high level of support in the same states. They therefore tended to support moves to increase the decision-making powers of the European Parliament and to modify the voting procedures of the Council of Ministers so as to eliminate the veto, moves which Britain consistently opposed.

The sole exception to this British opposition was the Thatcher Government's agreement to the majority-voting procedures of the Single European Act, which were specifically designed to allow the implementation of the single market (1992) programme. On other issues connected with the 1992 programme, though, the Thatcher Government's line was consistent with that of its predecessors in supporting a view of European integration as being about economic deregulation with the addition of co-operation between sovereign states on foreign policy.

This minimalist view was in line with the general perception of the British public on the subject. If anything, public opinion was less favourable to even the minimalist view of integration than was elite opinion. Whether this was a constraint on policy, or a consequence of policy is an open question. It was probably a combination of the two. By the end of the 1980s, though, there were signs of a shift in public opinion that was not being entirely reflected in the continued negativism of the tone of British government policy, especially as expressed by the Prime Minister. With the development by the Labour Party of a more positive stance on the issue, European integration had moved into a high position on the domestic political agenda.

The risk that Britain might be left behind in the moves to create a single market with a single currency was at the root of this new concern. But as the 1990s began it was no longer as clear as it had been a year earlier that the other EC states were going to move rapidly down that path. Events in Eastern Europe had shock waves that threatened to take the momentum out of the 1992 programme, and perhaps implied a new relevance for the minimalist British view of European integration.

Mrs Thatcher argued that the need to bring the East European states into a close relationship with, and perhaps even membership of the EC meant that there should be less talk of monetary union and centralized decision-making. She argued that these states, having just recovered their sovereign independence after an era of domination by the Soviet Union would not be keen to surrender it to Brussels.

Against that view Jacques Delors argued that the implication of the freeing of Eastern Europe was the exact opposite: he believed that it implied the need for more rapid progress on all aspects of the 1992 programme, including monetary union and the centralizing of decision-making. Without such steps, he believed, the EC would be torn apart by the historical requirement to forge a relationship with East Europe.

Perhaps Thatcher and Delors had essentially the same view of the effect of Eastern Europe on the process of integration: it was just that Thatcher welcomed the idea that the process would no longer drive forward to closer union, whereas Delors regretted it.

In the meantime the degree of integration that had already been achieved was having more far-reaching effects on the constitutional, political, economic, social, and environmental dimensions of life in contemporary Britain than had been envisaged when the applications for British membership were made in the 1960s and early 1970s. Whether those effects would increase depended at the time of writing on whose view of the implications of the East European developments for European integration proved to be the more influential: that of Jacques Delors or that of Margaret Thatcher.

Outline Chronology

March 1948	Brussels Treaty
May 1948	Hague Congress
April 1949	North Atlantic Treaty Setting up Nato
May 1949	Statute of Council of Europe
May 1950	Schuman Plan for a European Coal and Steel Community
October 1950	Pleven Plan for a European Defence Community
April 1951	Treaty of Paris creating European Coal and Steel Community
May 1952	Treaty to create a European Defence Community
August 1954	European Defence Community Treaty refused ratification by French National Assembly
October 1954	Treaty creating Western European Union
June 1955	Messina Conference begins
March 1957	Treaties of Rome creating European Atomic Energy Community and European Economic Community
May 1960	European Free Trade Association comes into operation
	Agreement between EEC states to accelerate progress on creating common market

November 1961	Fouchet Plan
January 1963	French veto of British application for membership
July 1965	French begin boycott of Community institutions
January 1966	Luxembourg compromise
July 1967	Merger of the three Communities
December 1967	Second French veto of British membership
December 1969	Hague summit
January 1972	Treaty of Accession signed by Britain and other applicants
January 1973	Britain becomes a member of EC
March 1979	Start of European Monetary System
June 1979	First direct elections to European Parliament
January 1981	Greece becomes tenth member of EC
November 1981	Genscher-Colombo Plan to revitalize EC discussed at London European Council
June 1983	Stuttgart European Council issues Solemn Declaration on European Union
February 1984	European Paliament adopts draft Treaty of European Union
June 1984	Fontainebleau European Council settles British budgetary dispute
January 1986	Spain and Portugal become members of the EC
July 1987	Single European Act comes into operation

Bibliography

Bailey, Richard (1983) *The European Connection* (Oxford, Pergamon).

Barker, Elisabeth (1971) *Britain in a Divided Europe* (London, Weidenfeld & Nicolson).

Barker, Elisabeth (1983) *The British Between the Superpowers, 1945–50* (London, Macmillan).

Bilski, Raphaella (1977) 'The Common Market and the growing strength of Labour's left wing', *Government and Opposition* 12, pp. 306–31.

Bodenheimer, Susanne J. (1967) *Political Union: A Microcosm of European Politics, 1960–1966* (Leyden, A.W. Sijthoff).

Brew, David (1979) 'National Parliamentary Scrutiny of European Legislation: the Case of the United Kingdom', in Valentine Herman and Rinus van Schendelen (eds) *The European Parliament and the National Parliaments* (Farnborough, Saxon House) pp. 238–78.

Bulpitt, Jim (1988) 'Rational Politicians and Conservative Statecraft in the Open Polity', in Peter Byrd (ed.), *British Foreign Policy under Thatcher* (Oxford, Philip Allen) pp. 180–205.

Burgess, Simon and Edwards, Geoffrey (1988) 'The Six plus One: British policy-making and the question of European economic integration, 1955', *International Affairs* 64, pp. 393–413.

Camps, Miriam (1964) *Britain and the European Community:*

1955–63 (London, Oxford University Press).

Carlton, David (1981) *Anthony Eden: A Biography* (London, Allen Lane).

Charlton, Michael (1983) *The Price of Victory* (London, British Broadcasting Corporation).

Collins, Doreen (1983) 'Social Policy', in Juliet Lodge (ed.), *Institutions and Policies of the European Community* (London, Frances Pinter) pp. 97–109.

Coombes, David (1970) *Politics and Bureaucracy in the European Community: A Portrait of the Commission of the E.E.C.* (London, Allen & Unwin).

Diebold, William (1959) *The Schuman Plan* (New York, Praeger).

Eden, Anthony (1960) *Memoirs. Full Circle* (London, Cassell).

Foot, Michael (1975) 'Putting Parliament at stake', *The Times*, 23 May.

Frankel, Joseph (1975) *British Foreign Policy, 1945–1973* (London, Oxford University Press).

Freestone, David (1983) 'The European Court of Justice', in Juliet Lodge (ed.) *Institutions and Policies of the European Community* (London, Frances Pinter) pp. 43–53.

Fursdon, Edward (1980) *The European Defence Community: A History* (London, Macmillan).

Gallup Poll (1989) *The Image of Europe* (London, Social Surveys (Gallup Poll) Ltd.).

Garavaglio, Guido (1984) 'From Rambouillet to Williamsburg: A Historical Assessment', in Cesar Merlini (ed.), *Economic Summits and Western Decision-Making* (London, Croom Helm).

Gardner, Nick (1987) *Decade of Discontent. The Changing British Economy since 1973* (Oxford, Basil Blackwell).

George, Stephen (1980) 'The Sovereignty of Parliament and European Community Law', *International Affairs* 56, pp. 94–7.

George, Stephen (1985) *Politics and Policy in the European Community* (Oxford, Clarendon Press).

George, Stephen (1989) 'Britain and the European Community', *Contemporary Record*, 2, no. 5, pp. 15–17.

George, Stephen (1990) *An Awkward Partner: Britain in the European Community* (Oxford, Oxford University Press).

Grahl, John and Teague, Paul (1988) 'The British Labour

Party and the European Community', *Political Quarterly*, 59, pp. 72–85.

Gregory F.E.C. (1973) *Dilemmas of Government: Britain and the European Community* (Oxford, Martin Robertson).

Harrison, R. J. (1974) *Europe in Question: Theories of Regional International Intergration* (London, Allen & Unwin).

Hodges, Michael and Wallace, William (eds) (1981) *Economic Divergence in the European Community* (London, Royal Institute of International Affairs/Allen & Unwin).

Holt, Stephen (1973) 'Policy-Making in Practice – The 1965 Crisis', in James Barber and Bruce Reed (eds), *European Community: Vision and Reality* (London, Croom Helm) pp. 66–73.

Hornsby, Michael (1978) 'How Britain loses out when they balance the books in Brussels', *The Times*, 11 August.

Hu, Yao-su (1981) *Europe under Stress: Convergence and Divergence in the European Community* (London, Royal Institute of International Affairs/Butterworths).

Kitzinger, Uwe (1973) *Diplomacy and Persuasion: How Britain Joined the Common Market*, (London, Thames and Hudson).

Kolinsky, Martin (1975) Parliamentary Scrutiny of European Legislation, *Government and Opposition*, 10, 1975, pp. 46–69.

Laurent, Pierre-Henri (1972) 'The Diplomacy of the Rome Treaty', *Journal of Contemporary History*, 7, pp. 209–20.

Lindberg, Leon N. (1963) *The Political Dynamics of European Economic Integration* (London, Oxford University Press).

Lipgens, Walter (1982) *A History of European Integration. Volume 1, 1945–1947: The Formation of the European Unity Movement* (Oxford, Clarendon Press).

Lodge, Juliet (ed.) (1986) *European Union: the European Community in Search of a Future* (London, Macmillan).

Lodge, Juliet (1989) 'The European Parliament–from "assembly" to co-legislature: changing the institutional dynamics', in Juliet Lodge (ed.) *The European Community and the Challenge of the Future* (London, Pinter) pp. 58–79.

Ludlow, Peter (1982) *The Making of the European Monetary System. A case study of the politics of the European Community* (London, Butterworth).

Macmillan, Harold (1971) *Riding the Storm, 1956–1959* (London, Macmillan).

Martin, David (1988) *Bringing common sense to the Common Market: a left agenda for Europe* (London, Fabian Society Tract no. 525).

McKinlay, R.D. and Little, R. (1986) *Global Problems and World Order* (London, Frances Pinter).

Milward, Alan (1984) *The Reconstruction of Western Europe, 1945–51* (London, Methuen).

Mitchell, J.D.B. (1979) 'The Sovereignty of Parliament and Community Law: The Stumbling Block That Isn't There' *International Affairs*, 55, pp. 33–46.

Monnet, Jean (1963) 'A Ferment of Change', *Journal of Common Market Studies*, 1, 1962–3, pp. 203–11.

Monnet, Jean (1978) *Memoirs* (translated by Richard Mayne) (London, Collins).

Morgan, Annette (1976) *From Summit to Council: Evolution in the EEC* (London, Chatham House/PEP).

Morgan, Kenneth O. (1984) *Labour in Power, 1945–1951* (Oxford, Clarendon Press).

Morse, Edward L. (1973) 'Crisis diplomacy: the demise of the Smithsonian agreement', *The World Today*, 29, pp. 243–56.

Newman, Michael (1983) *Socialism and European Unity: The Dilemma of the Left in Britain and France* (London, Junction Books).

Nugent, Neill (1989) *The Government and Politics of the European Community* (London, Macmillan)

Pelkmans, Jacques and Winters, Alan (1988) *Europe's Domestic Market* (London, Royal Institute of International Affairs/Routledge).

Pierce, Roy, Valen, Henry and Listhaug, Ola (1983) 'Referendum Voting Behavior: The Norwegian and British Referenda on Membership in the European Community', *American Journal of Political Science*, 27, pp. 43–63.

Porter, Bernard (1983) *Britain, Europe and the world, 1850–1982: Delusions of Grandeur* (London, Allen & Unwin).

Powell, J. Enoch (1975) 'The one stark fact that goes beyond butter mountains and bureaucrats' *The Times*, 4 June.

Robins, L.J. (1979) *The Reluctant Party: Labour and the EEC, 1961–75* (Ormskirk, G.W. & A. Hesketh).

Rosamond, Ben (1990) 'Labour and the European Community: Learning to be European?' *Politics*, 10, pp. 25–32.

Sampson, Anthony (1967) *Macmillan. A Study in Ambiguity* (London, Allen Lane).

Schermers, H.G. (1974) 'The European Court of Justice: Promoter of European Integration', *American Journal of Comparative Law* 22, pp. 444–64.

Schlesinger, Arthur M. Jr. (1965) *A Thousand Days: John F. Kennedy in the White House* (London, Andre Deutsch).

Shlaim, Avi, Jones, Peter and Sainsbury, Keith (1977) *British Foreign Secretaries since 1945* (Newton Abbot, David and Charles).

Silj, Alessandro (1967) *Europe's Political Puzzle: A Study of the Fouchet Negotiations and the 1963 Veto* (Cambridge, Mass., Harvard University Center for International Affairs, Occasional Papers in International Affairs number 17).

Smith, David (1987) 'Growing trade with our partners in Europe' *The Times* 4 February.

Spaak, Paul-Henri (1971) *The Continuing Battle: Memoirs of a European, 1936–1966*, translated from the French by Henry Fox (London, Weidenfeld and Nicolson).

Statler, Jocelyn (1979) 'British Foreign Policy to 1985. The European monetary system: from conception to birth' *International Affairs*, 55, pp. 206–25.

Steel, David (1980) *A House Divided: The Lib-Lab Pact and the Future of British Politics* (London, Weidenfeld & Nicolson).

Steiner, Josephine (1990) *Textbook on EEC Law*, (London, Blackstone).

Story, Jonathan (1988) 'The Launching of the EMS: An Analysis of Change in Foreign Economic Policy' *Political Studies*, 26, pp. 397–412.

Thatcher, Margaret (1988) *Britain and Europe: Text of the speech delivered in Bruges by the Prime Minister on 20th September 1988* (London, Conservative Political Centre).

Tsoukalis, Loukas (1977) *The Politics and Economics of European Monetary Integration* (London, Allen & Unwin).

Urwin, D.W. (1981) *Western Europe since 1945: A Short Political History* (London, Longman, 3rd edition).

Wallace, William (1984) *Britain's Bilateral Links Within Western Europe* (London, Royal Institute of International Affairs/ Routledge & Kegan Paul).

Whitehead, Phillip (1977) 'Dithering over Direct Elections', *New Statesman*, 4 March, pp. 275–6.

Williams, Shirley (1975) 'Our friends abroad cannot all be wrong in wanting us to stay in the EEC', *The Times*, 27 May.

Wilson, Harold (1979) *Final Term: The Labour Government, 1974–6* (London, Weidenfeld & Nicolson and Michael Joseph).

Young, John W. (1984) *Britain, France and the Unity of Europe* (Leicester, Leicester University Press).

Young, Simon Z. (1973) *Terms of Entry: Britain's Negotiations with the European Community, 1970–1972* (Heinemann, London).

Index